contents

"Every string is a different color, a different voice."
—Andres Segovia, *Christian Science Monitor*, August 5, 1986

I have always found colorwork irresistible. Charming vintage knitting patterns with pony-tailed ladies sipping their après-ski toddies live in my knitter's heart right next to the memory of my first baby bootie and the day I finally executed a tubular cast-on. Cables cajole me into their braided embrace, lace lures me beneath its weightless impossibility, and knitting of all stripes has at one time or other held my attention, but I always seem to wander back home to colorwork.

When I made my first halting stitches with not one, but two strings on my sticks, I was captivated. Not having been blessed with a Scandinavian Aunty, or any friend who could show me the path to pattern, I sought out formal instruction. Enrolling in a Norwegian knitting class at my local yarn shop, I learned how to hold the strands, how to create a steek, and horror of horrors, how to cut up the front of my masterpiece with shears! After that class, I was emboldened to attempt even braver feats of fiber. I voraciously read all I could find about stranded knitting, experimenting with every new technique. These methods were noticeably absent from the colorwork patterns I could readily find. They all contained enigmatic instructions like "working back and forth . . ." I thought I was knitting in the round! How can I purl back and maintain this pattern in reverse? Then came the finishing. I suspected that no one discussed finishing Norwegian sweaters much because no one ever had finished one, Scandinavian Aunties excepted.

I stumbled ahead though, always adoring the feel of the wool. I found the rhythmic repetition of the patterns hypnotic. I began to see tubular construction techniques as more logical and easier than flat knitting with seams. I started to intuit the way the puzzle-tubes fit together. I was besotted with combination upon combination of color. I strayed far away from traditional patterns, creating orca whales and tree frogs, sunflowers and motorbikes, all in chart form. At first this was only to amuse myself while I continued my assault on the mysteries of the translated pattern. But then my friends at local knitting shops began to ask me for designs that were special for their customers, for charts that were logical and easy to read, and to teach them what I had learned. One fine day I realized that a book was born of my odyssey, and I couldn't wait to share it.

I hope you will enjoy this collection, both using its designs and creating your own. Never feel bound to any rule that doesn't suit you or your knitting. *The New Stranded Colorwork* is folk art, not masterwork. It speaks of the everyday things that have meaning to everyday people like you and me, and probably to some Scandinavian Aunties, too.

"I know of the leafy paths that the witches take / Who come with their crowns of pearl and their spindles of wool . . ."

—William Butler Yeats

Sometimes as knitters, we get caught up in overcomplicating things. We want to challenge ourselves; we want to get just the right fit, to explore new silhouettes, to push the envelope of our own expectations. That can be a lot to expect from ourselves, and our creations. Often the simplest shapes turn out to be the most pleasing, and, certainly, they provide the best canvases for color. This hat is a good balance between structure and decoration. Its shape is uncluttered, leaving plenty of quiet where the strands of color can sing. Take a walk down your own leafy path. Be still and listen to the music of the trees.

leafy toque

FINISHED SIZE

About 19¾" (50 cm) head circumference and 6¾" (17 cm) tall. To fit a child (see Note on page 8).

YARN

Fingering weight (#1 Super Fine).
Shown here: Rauma Babygarn (100% superwash wool; 190 yd [174 m]/50 g): #63 forest heather (MC), #11 cream (CC1), #150 old gold (CC2), #13 gray heather (CC3), and #43 copper (CC4), 1 ball each.

NEEDLES

Size U.S. 2 (2.75 mm): set of 4 or 5 double-pointed (dpn). Adjust needle size if necessary to obtain the correct gauge.

NOTIONS

Marker (m); tapestry needle.

GAUGE

33 stitches and 38 rounds = 4" (10 cm) in charted pattern, worked in rounds.

- ■ MC
- | CC1
- ◿ CC2
- + CC3
- ◣ CC4
- ☐ pattern repeat

Leaf Border

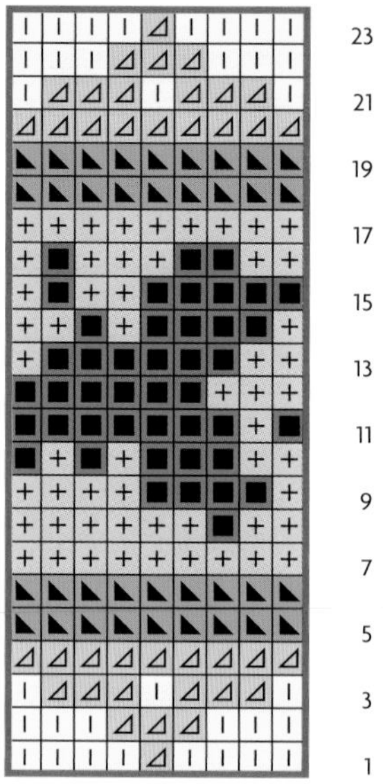

Crown

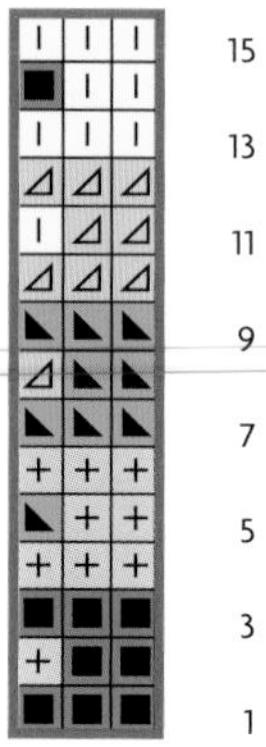

STITCH GUIDE

Corrugated Ribbing (multiple of 2 sts)

Set-up rnd: *K1 with MC, k1 with CC4; rep from *.

Rnd 1: *K1 with MC, p1 with CC4; rep from *.

Rep Rnd 1 for patt.

Note

Adjust the circumference by adding or subtracting 9-stitch pattern repeats. One repeat measures about 1" (2.5 cm). Adjust the length by adding or subtracting stripes in the Crown chart before beginning crown shaping.

HAT

With MC, and using the tubular 1x1 method (see Glossary), CO 162 sts. Arrange sts as evenly as possible on 3 or 4 needles, place marker (pm), and join for working in rnds, being careful not to twist sts. Join CC4 and work in corrugated rib (see Stitch Guide) for 6 rnds. Knit 1 rnd with MC. Work Rows 1–23 of Leaf Border chart. Work Rows 1–15 of Crown chart—piece measures about 4¾" (12 cm) from CO.

Shape Crown

Work Rows 1–15 of Crown chart once more, then cont with MC only and *at the same time* shape top as foll:

Rnd 1: *K7, k2tog; rep from *—144 sts rem.
Rnd 2 and all even-numbered rnds: Knit.
Rnd 3: *K6, k2tog; rep from *—126 sts rem.
Rnd 5: *K5, k2tog; rep from *—108 sts rem.
Rnd 7: *K4, k2tog; rep from *—90 sts rem.
Rnd 9: *K3, k2tog; rep from *—72 sts rem.
Rnd 11: *K2, k2tog; rep from *—54 sts rem.
Rnd 13: *K1, k2tog; rep from *—36 sts rem.
Rnds 15 and 17: *K2tog; rep from *—9 sts rem after Rnd 17.
Rnd 19: *K3tog; rep from *—3 sts rem.
Work 3-st I-cord (see Glossary) for ½" (1.3 cm).

FINISHING

Break yarn, leaving an 8" (20.5 cm) tail. Thread tail on a tapestry needle and pull through rem 3 sts, pull tight to close hole, and fasten off to WS. Weave in loose ends. Block to measurements.

Examine this book and others for charts that are interchangeable or create your own using graph paper. Just count the number of stitches in each repeat and work accordingly.

"When winds go organing through the pines
On hill and headland, darkly gleaming,
Meseems I hear sonorous lines
Of Iliads that the woods are dreaming."
— Madison Cawein, *The Wind in the Pines*

timberline

FINISHED SIZE
39½ (44¼, 49¼)" (100.5 [112.5, 125] cm) chest circumference. Sweater shown measures 44¼" (112.5 cm).

YARN
Sportweight (#2 Fine).
Shown here: Rauma Finullgarn (100% wool; 180 yd [165 m]/50 g): #403 light grey heather (MC), 7 (8, 9) balls; #486 dark olive green (CC1), 1 (1, 2) ball(s); #434 burnt orange (CC2) and #428 cranberry red (CC3), 1 ball each for all sizes.

NEEDLES
Body and sleeves: size U.S. 3 (3.25 mm): 24" (60 cm) circular (cir) and set of 4 or 5 double-pointed (dpn).
Facing: size U.S. 2 (2.75 mm): 24" (60 cm) cir and set of 4 or 5 dpn. Adjust needle size if necessary to obtain the correct gauge.

NOTIONS
Stitch holders or waste yarn; marker (m); tapestry needle; sharp-point sewing needle and matching thread; six ⅞" (2.2 cm) buttons.

GAUGE
26 stitches and 37 rounds = 4" (10 cm) in stockinette stitch on larger needle, worked in rounds.

This sweater is my idea of a perfect first stranded colorwork project. You may have tried a hat or two and are getting the hang of handling the yarns, but you might not feel ready to slice up the front of a cardigan with your shears. Here is the next step: a simple pullover with almost no shaping, minimal cutting, and just enough colorwork to keep it interesting. You can do it; just head for the trees!

Large Trees

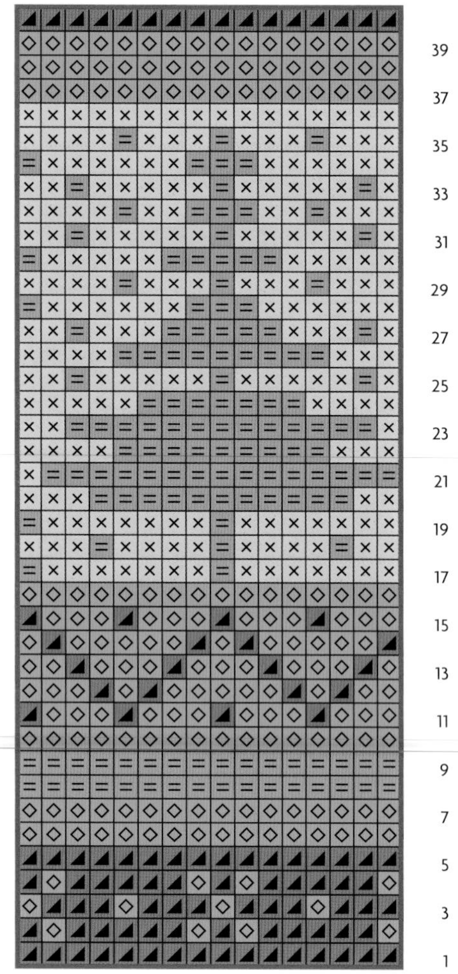

Small Trees

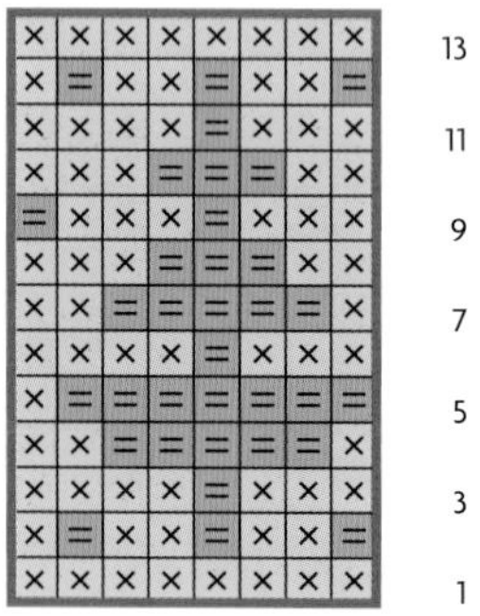

- × MC
- = CC1
- ◇ CC2
- ◢ CC3
- ☐ pattern repeat

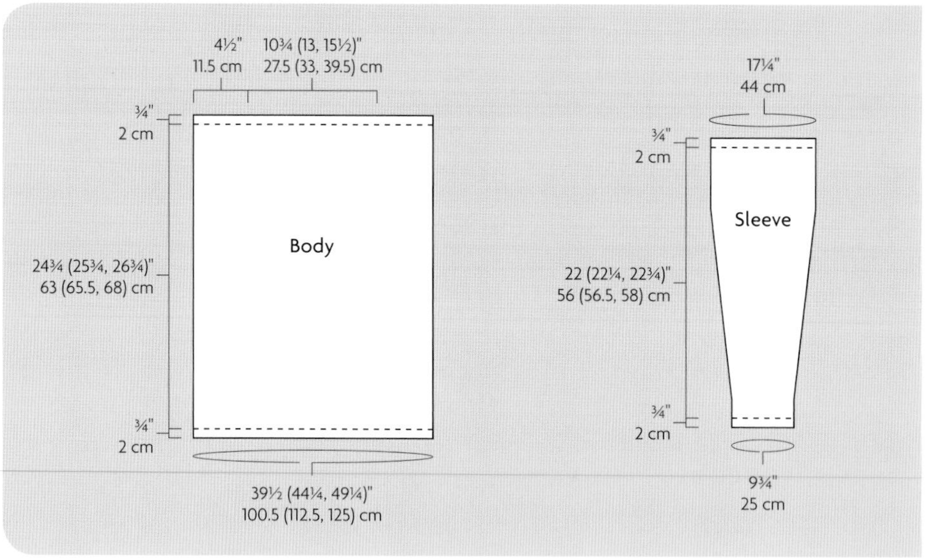

BODY

With MC and smaller cir needle, CO 256 (288, 320) sts. Place marker (pm) and join for working in rnds, being careful not to twist sts. Knit 6 rnds. Change to CC3 and knit 1 rnd, then purl 1 rnd for turning ridge. Change to larger cir needle and knit 1 rnd. Change to CC2 and knit 3 rnds. Change to MC and knit 2 rnds. Work Rows 1–13 of Small Trees chart. Cont even in MC until piece measures 20 (21, 22)" (51 [53.5, 56] cm) from turning ridge. Work Rows 1–40 of Large Trees chart. Change to smaller needle. With CC3, purl 1 rnd for turning ridge. Knit 1 rnd.

Facing

BO 3 sts for half of top of left armhole, work 122 (138, 154) sts in k1, p1 rib, BO next 6 sts for top of right armhole, work 122 (138, 154) sts in k1, p1 rib and place these sts on holder or waste yarn, BO rem 3 sts for other half of top of left armhole—122 (138, 154) sts rem each for front and back. Break yarn. With RS facing, rejoin CC3 to front sts. Working back and forth in rows, work in established rib for 4 more rows. BO all sts in patt. With RS facing, rejoin CC3 to held sts and work in k1, p1 rib for 4 rows. BO all sts in patt.

SLEEVES (make 2)

With MC and smaller dpn, CO 64 sts for all sizes. Arrange sts evenly on 3 or 4 dpn, pm, and join for working in rnds, being careful not to twist sts. Knit 6 rnds. Change to CC3 and knit 1 rnd. Purl 1 rnd for turning ridge. Change to larger dpn and knit 1 rnd. Change to CC2 and knit 3 rnds. Change to MC and knit 2 rnds. Work Rows 1–13 of Small Trees chart. Cont with MC, inc 1 st each side of m on next rnd, then every foll 6th rnd 23 more times—112 sts. Work even until piece measures 17¼ (17½, 18)" (44 [44.5, 45.5] cm) from turning ridge. Work Rows 1–40 of Large Trees chart. With CC3, knit 1 rnd. With MC, purl 6 rnds for facing, inc 1 st each side of m every rnd. Loosely BO all sts.

FINISHING

Weave in loose ends. Block pieces to measurements.

Facing and Hems

Turn body facing to WS along turning ridge and, with sharp-point sewing needle and matching thread, sew in place. Turn lower body and sleeve hems to WS and, with sharp-point sewing needle and matching thread, sew in place.

Cut Armholes

Mark, machine stitch, and cut armhole openings as described on pages 125–127.

Overlap upper folded edges ½" (1.3 cm) at shoulder and tack together through armhole edges with sharp-point sewing needle and matching thread. Insert sleeves into armholes and sew in place as described on page 132, stitching through all layers at upper edge overlap. Fold sleeve facing to WS to cover cut edges of openings and, with sharp-point sewing needle and matching thread, sew in place. Sew 3 buttons to each front shoulder, placing the first 1" (2.5 cm) from armhole edge, the second 4½" (11.5 cm) from armhole edge, and the third evenly spaced between. Make 3 button loops on each back shoulder edge opposite buttons as foll: Join CC3 to shoulder. Make a loop of CC3 large enough to accommodate button; take a st in shoulder to secure. Work buttonhole st (see Glossary) over loop to strengthen. Rep for rem buttons.

"It is the size of the owner's heart and brain and goodwill that make his garden either delightful or dull."

—Gertrude Jekyll

The inspiration for a project can sometimes come when you aren't looking for it. An explosive flowerbed, a pile of children's toys, or even, as in this case, the singular hue on the walls of a dear friend's music room. I can hear her fiddle playing still . . .

kjersten

FINISHED SIZE

30¾ (34¾, 38¾)" (78 [88.5, 98.5] cm) chest circumference. Sweater shown measures 34¾" (88.5 cm).

YARN

Sportweight (#2 Fine).

Shown here: Brown Sheep Nature Spun Sport (100% wool; 184 yd [168 m]/50 g): #144 limestone (green; MC) and #601 pepper (black; CC1), 4 (4, 5) balls each; #105 bougainvillea (red; CC2) and #N54 orange you glad (CC3), 1 ball each for all sizes.

NEEDLES

Body and sleeves: size U.S. 4 (3.5 mm): 24" (60 cm) circular (cir) and set of 4 or 5 double-pointed (dpn). *Hem facings:* size U.S. 3 (3.25 mm): 24" (60 cm) cir and set of 4 or 5 dpn. Adjust needle size if necessary to obtain the correct gauge.

NOTIONS

Stitch holders or waste yarn; markers (m); tapestry needle; sharp-point sewing needle and matching thread; seven 2" (5 cm) pewter hook closures; 1¾ yd (1.6 m) of ¾" (2 cm) black velvet trim (optional).

GAUGE

28 stitches and 30 rounds = 4" (10 cm) in charted pattern on larger needle, worked in rounds.

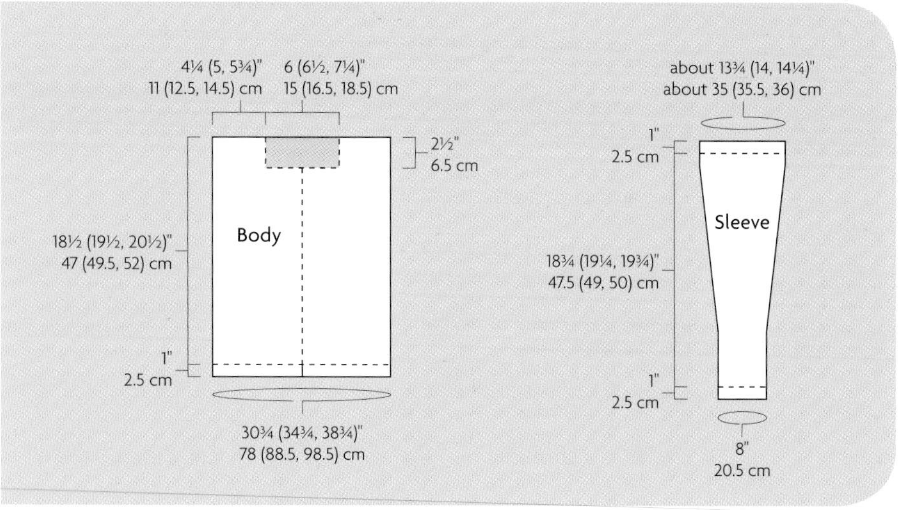

△ MC

■ CC1

+ CC3

☐ pattern repeat

Stripes

Lower Body

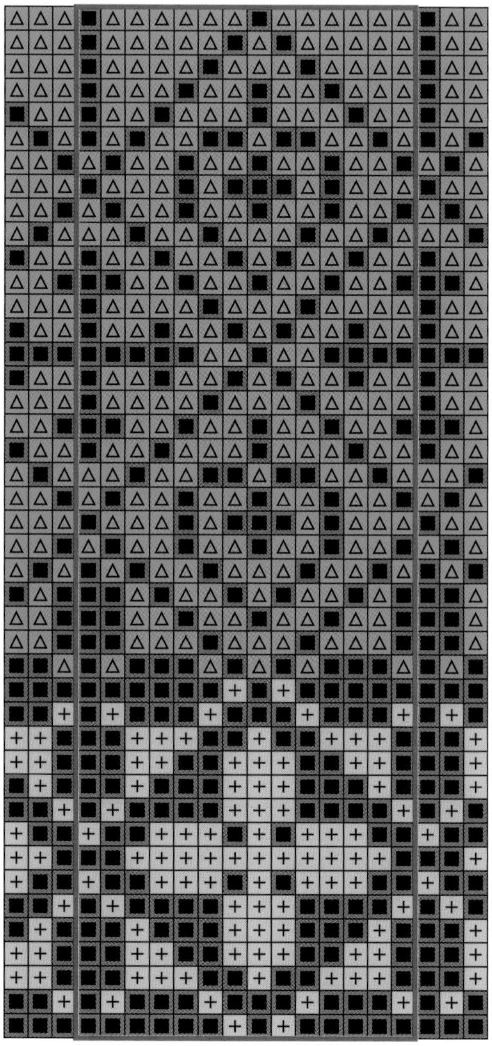

BODY

With CC2 and smaller cir needle, CO 216 (244, 272) sts. Do not join. Work back and forth in St st for 7 rows. **Picot row:** (WS) *K2tog, yo; rep from * to last 2 sts, k2tog—1 st dec'd. Change to larger cir needle. Knit 1 row, inc 1 st at beg of row—1 st inc'd. **Joining row:** Place marker (pm), use the backward-loop method (see Glossary) to CO 6 sts for steek (see page 124; these sts are not included in st count unless otherwise indicated), pm, join for working in rnds, being careful not to twist sts, knit to end of rnd. Work Rows 1–43 of Lower Body chart. Rep Row 1 of Stripes chart until piece measures 12 (13, 14)" (30.5 [33, 35.5] cm) from picot row. Work Rows 1–47 of Hearts chart (see page 18).

Place Stitches on Holders

With CC1 and beg at center of front steek, BO 3 steek sts, k21 (23, 25) and place these sts on a holder for right center front, k30 (35, 40) and place these sts on another holder for right front shoulder, BO the next 6 sts for top of right armhole, k30 (35, 40) and place these sts on another holder for right back shoulder, k42 (46, 50) and place these sts on another holder for back neck, k30 (35, 40) and place these sts on another holder for left back shoulder, BO the next 6 sts for top of left armhole, k30 (35, 40) and place these sts on another holder for left front shoulder, k21 (23, 25) and place these sts on another holder for left center front, BO rem 3 steek sts.

Lower Sleeve

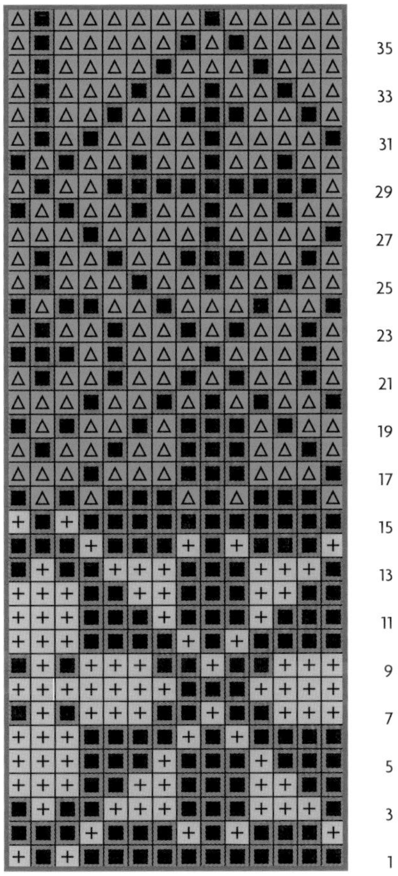

SLEEVES (make 2)

With CC2 and smaller dpn, CO 56 sts. Pm and join for working in rnds, being careful not to twist sts. Work 7 rnds in St st. **Picot rnd:** *K2tog, yo; rep from *. Change to larger dpn and knit 2 more rnds. Work Rows 1–36 of Lower Sleeve chart. Rep Row 36 of Lower Sleeve chart, inc 1 st each side of marker every 5th rnd, working new sts into patt, until piece measures 12½ (13, 13½)" (31.5 [33, 34.5] cm) from picot rnd. Cont to inc every 5th rnd, work Rows 1–47 of Hearts chart, aligning vertical CC1 lines of chart with CC1 stripes on sleeve. With CC1, purl 6 rnds for facing, inc 1 st each side of marker every rnd. Loosely BO all sts.

FINISHING

Block pieces to measurements. Mark, machine stitch, and cut center front steek and armhole openings as described on pages 125–127. Mark, machine stitch, and cut square front neckline to a depth of 2½" (6.5 cm) as described on page 129. Place 30 (35, 40) held right front shoulder sts on one needle and corresponding 30 (35, 40) right back shoulder sts on another needle. With RS tog, use the three-needle method as described on page 130 to BO the shoulder sts tog. Rep for other shoulder.

Hearts

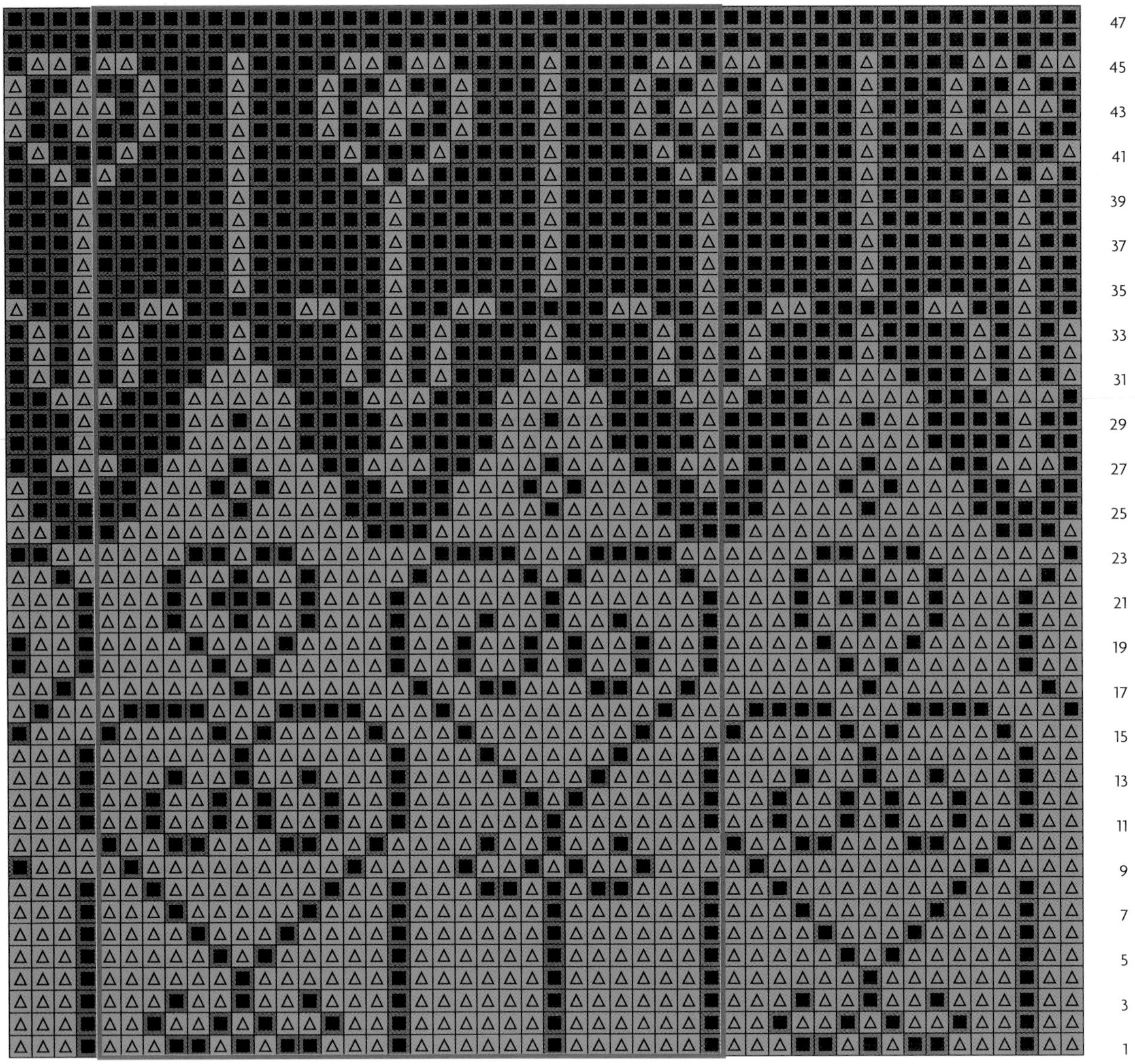

△ MC

■ CC1

\+ CC3

☐ pattern repeat

When knitting vertical stripes, pay close attention to keeping floats loose. Floats that are too tight will cause unsightly vertical ridges. If you are in doubt, make your floats looser than you think they should be.

Hems

Fold each hem to WS along picot row. With sharp-point sewing needle and matching thread, sew in place.

Front Bands

With CC2, smaller needle, and RS facing, pick up and knit 88 (94, 100) sts along right front edge between steek and body sts. Beg and end with a WS row, work in St st for 5 rows. Purl 1 RS row for turning ridge. Work 5 more rows in St st. Loosely BO all sts. Fold band to WS along turning ridge. With sharp-point sewing needle and matching thread, sew band in place. Rep for left front edge.

Neckband

With CC2, smaller needle, and RS facing, pick up and knit 22 (24, 26) sts along center right front neck edge, pm, 16 sts along right neck slope, pm, k42 (46, 50) held back neck sts, pm, pick up and knit 16 sts along left neck slope, pm, and 22 (24, 26) sts along center left front neck—118 (126, 134) sts total. Purl 1 WS row. **Dec row:** (RS) *Knit to 2 sts before m, ssk, slip marker (sl m), k2tog; rep from * 3 more times, knit to end of row—8 sts dec'd. Purl 1 WS row. Rep dec row—102 (110, 118) sts rem. **Picot row:** *P2tog, yo; rep from * to last 2 sts, p2tog—1 st dec'd. **Inc row:** (RS) *Knit to m, M1 (see Glossary), sl m, M1; rep from * 3 more times, knit to end of row—8 sts inc'd. Purl 1 WS row. Rep inc row—117 (125, 133) sts. Purl 1 WS row. Loosely BO all sts. Fold neckband to WS along picot row. With sharp-point sewing needle and matching thread, sew in place.

With sharp-point sewing needle and matching thread, sew optional ribbon trim to front and neck edges, forming miters at the corners to reduce bulk. Sew closures to front, placing the highest just below neckband, the lowest just above picot edge, and the others evenly spaced in between.

Insert sleeves into armholes and sew in place as described on page 132. Fold sleeve facings to WS to cover cut edges of openings and with sharp-point sewing needle and matching thread, sew in place.

Weave in loose ends. Block again if desired.

"Beautiful swimmers
Flash of gold and then you've gone
You know I'm watching"
—Ancient Haiku

being koi

Just as the depths of a fish pond contain countless hues, the many strands of color in Shetland wool are varied and complex. If you have ever spent time fish gazing by a real koi pond, you understand its contemplative and peaceful nature. Yarn lovers who have done so will support my assertion that Shetland wool is a pretty good alternative when you just can't get to a Japanese garden. This vest is a meditation on the nature of "complicated" color; an invitation to pause awhile and drink in both the muted and the strident filaments contained in its wool. "Yarn" is a synonym for "story." What kind of tale could these fish tell?

FINISHED SIZE

30¾ (34¼, 37¾)" (78 [87, 96] cm) chest circumference. Vest shown measures 34¼" (87 cm).

YARN

Sportweight (#2 Fine).
Shown here: Harrisville Designs New England Shetland (100% wool; 217 yd [198 m]/50 g): #038 teak (MC), 3 (3, 4) skeins; #040 topaz (CC1), 1 (1, 2) skein(s); #013 peacock (CC2), #070 bluegrass (CC3), and #065 poppy (CC4), 1 skein each for all sizes.

NEEDLES

Body and ribbing: size U.S. 3 (3.25 mm): 24" (60 cm) circular (cir). *Facings:* size U.S. 2 (2.75 mm): 16" (40 cm) and 24" (60 cm) cir, and size U.S. 3 (3.25 mm): 16" (40 cm) cir. Adjust needle size if necessary to obtain the correct gauge.

NOTIONS

Stitch holders or waste yarn; markers (m); tapestry needle; sharp-point sewing needle and matching thread.

GAUGE

28 stitches and 33 rounds = 4" (10 cm) in charted pattern on larger needle, worked in rounds.

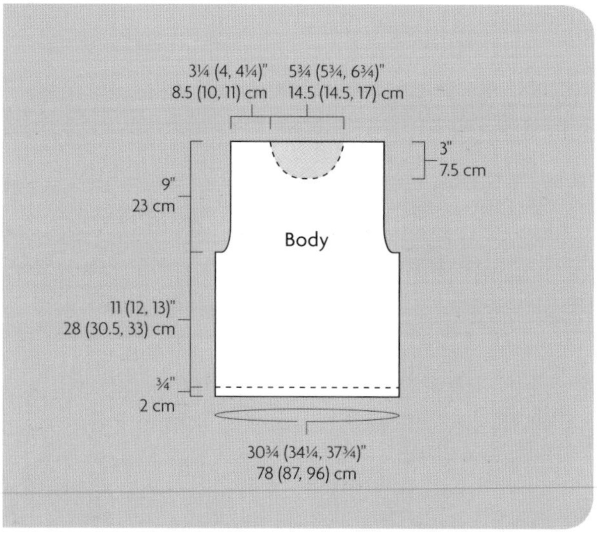

Dashes

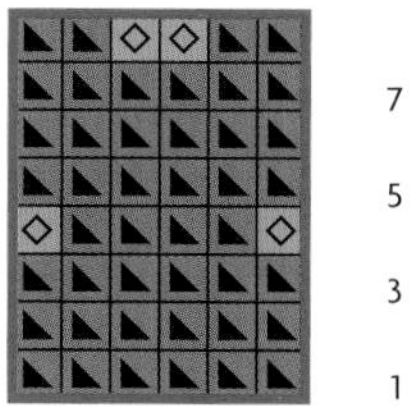

Reverse Dashes

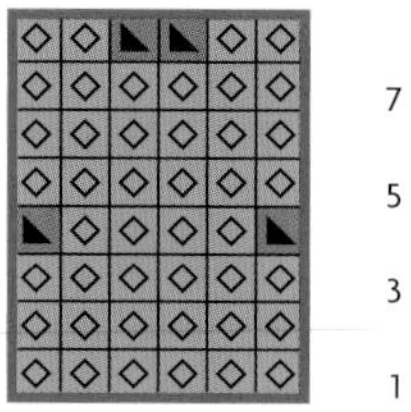

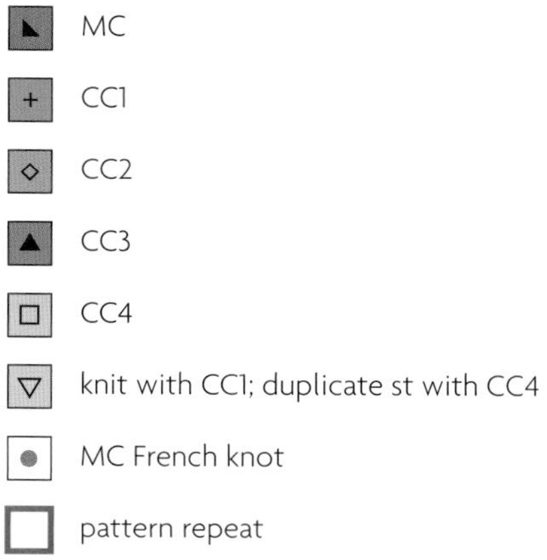

Fish

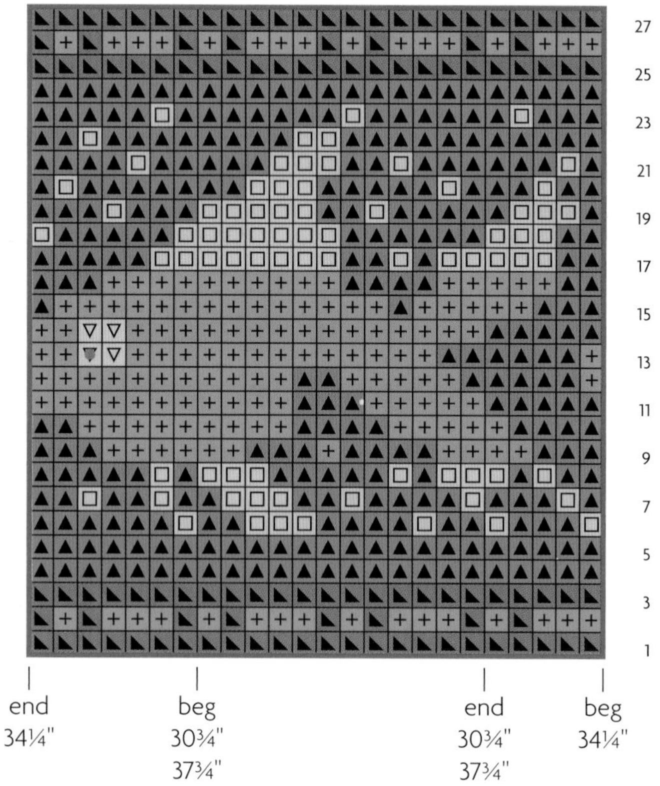

Accent

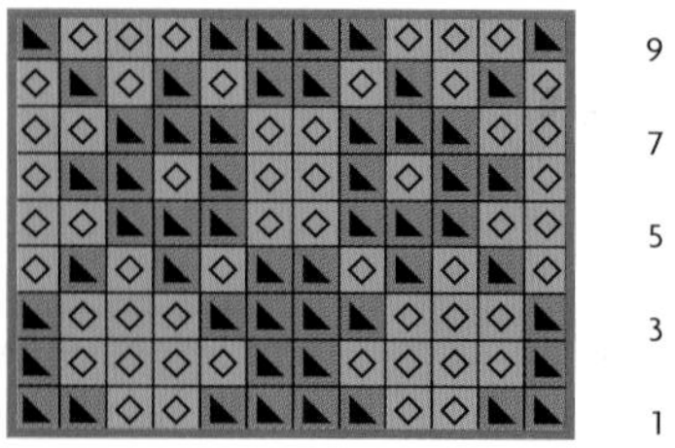

BODY

With MC and smaller cir needle, CO 216 (240, 264) sts. Place marker (pm) and join for working in rnds, being careful not to twist sts. Knit 6 rnds for facing. **Picot rnd:** *K2tog, yo; rep from *. Change to larger cir needle. Knit 6 rnds. **Next rnd:** *K2 with CC1, p2 with MC; rep from *. Rep last rnd until piece measures 6" (15 cm) from picot rnd. Rep Rows 1–8 of Dashes chart until piece measures 11 (12, 13)" (28 [30.5, 33] cm) from picot rnd.

Shape Armholes

Place the last 6 sts worked onto holder or waste yarn for left underarm, keeping in patt, work 6 sts, then place these 6 sts on the same holder for left underarm, work 96 (108, 120) sts in patt for front, work next 12 sts and place these 12 sts on holder or waste yarn for right underarm, work to end of rnd for back—96 (108, 120) sts each for front and back. **Next rnd:** Pm, use the backward-loop method (see Glossary) to CO 6 sts for armhole steek (see page 124; these sts are not included in st counts unless otherwise indicated), pm, work to next armhole in established patt, pm, CO 6 sts as before for armhole steek, pm, work to end of rnd in established patt. **Dec rnd:** Work 6 steek sts, work 3 sts in patt, ssk, work to 5 sts before armhole m, k2tog, work 3 sts, work 6 steek sts, work 3 sts, ssk, work to 5 sts before next armhole m, k2tog, work 3 sts—4 sts dec'd. Dec 1 st each side of each armhole steek in this manner every other rnd 5 more times—84 (96, 108) sts rem each for front and back. Work Rows 1–9 of Accent chart. Beg and end as indicated for your size, work Rows 1–27 of Fish chart. Work Rows 1–9 of Accent chart again. Rep Rows 1–8 of Reverse Dashes chart until piece measures 20 (21, 22)" (51 [53.5, 56] cm) from picot rnd.

Place Stitches on Holders

With CC2 and beg at center of left armhole steek, BO 3 steek sts, k22 (28, 30) and place these sts on a holder for left front shoulder, k40 (40, 48) and place these sts on a second holder for front neck, k22 (28, 30) and place these sts on a third holder for right front shoulder, BO 6 steek sts, k22 (28, 30) and place these sts on a fourth holder for right back shoulder, k40 (40, 48) and place these sts on a fifth holder for back neck, k22 (28, 30) and place these sts on a sixth holder for left back shoulder, BO 3 rem steek sts.

FINISHING

Block to measurements. Mark, machine stitch, and cut armhole steeks as described on pages 125–127. Turn lower facing to WS along picot rnd and with sharp-point sewing needle and matching thread, sew in place. With yarn threaded on a tapestry needle, work duplicate st and French knots (see Glossary) as indicated on Fish chart. Weave in loose ends.

Neckline

Mark, machine stitch, and cut front neckline curve to a depth of 3" (7.5 cm) as described on page 129. Join front to back at shoulders using the three-needle BO method as described on page 130. With MC, shorter larger cir needle, and RS facing, k40 (40, 48) held back neck sts, then pick up and knit 64 (64, 68) sts around front neck edge—104 (104, 116) sts total. Pm and join for working in rnds. Knit 6 rnds. **Picot rnd:** *K2tog, yo; rep from *. Change to shorter smaller cir needle and knit 6 rnds for facing. BO all sts. Fold facing to WS along picot rnd and sew in place.

Armbands

With MC, shorter larger cir needle, and RS facing, k12 held armhole sts, then pick up and knit 116 sts evenly spaced around armhole edge between steek and body sts—128 sts total. Pm and join for working in rnds. Knit 6 rnds. **Picot rnd:** *K2tog, yo; rep from *. Change to shorter smaller cir needle and knit 6 rnds for facing. BO all sts. Fold facing to WS along picot rnd and sew in place. Lightly steam bindings to block.

3456789

One for sorrow / Two for joy / Three for girls / Four for boys, / Five for silver / Six for gold / Seven for a secret never to be told / Eight for a wish / Nine for a kiss / Ten for a time of joyous bliss.

—Nursery Rhyme

counting crows

FINISHED SIZE

About 32 (36, 40)" (81.5 [91.5, 101.5] cm) chest circumference. Sweater shown measures 36" (91.5 cm).

YARN

Sportweight (#2 Fine).

Shown here: Dale of Norway Heilo (100% wool; 109 yd [100 m]/50 g): #4137 red (MC), 6 (7, 8) balls; #2434 tan (CC1) and #0090 black (CC2), 3 (4, 4) balls each.

NEEDLES

Body and sleeves: size U.S. 3 (3.25 mm): 24" (60 cm) circular (cir) and set of 4 or 5 double-pointed (dpn). *Edging:* size U.S. 2 (2.75 mm): 24" (60 cm) cir and set of 2 dpn. Adjust needle size if necessary to obtain the correct gauge.

NOTIONS

Stitch holders or waste yarn; markers (m); tapestry needle; sharp-point sewing needle and matching thread; five ¾" (2 cm) buttons.

GAUGE

24 stitches and 26 rounds = 4" (10 cm) in charted pattern on larger needle, worked in rounds.

I'll admit it: I'm a wee bit superstitious. Any time I see crows, I run through the rhyme in my head to see what sort of omen their number might portend. It's not that I really believe they can predict the future; it's more like buying lottery tickets, or reading horoscopes, or any of the other little things we humans are still doing to explain or anticipate our fortunes. It's in our nature to ascribe meaning to the creatures we share the planet with, to seek the comfort which attends explanation, and to somehow relate to black birds that steal shiny baubles and mate for life.

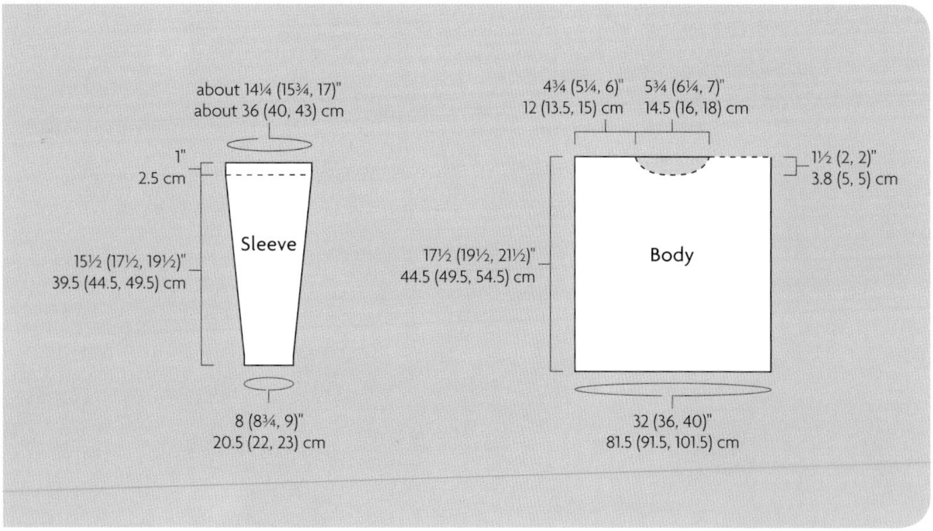

Use flower-head or lace pins when pinning pieces together. The large heads of these fine, sharp, snag-free pins won't catch on floats or disappear between stitches.

BODY

With CC1 and smaller dpn, CO 5 sts. Work 5-st I-cord (see Glossary) until piece measures 32 (36, 40)" (81.5 [91.5, 101.5] cm) from CO. Place sts on holder. With larger needle and MC, pick up and knit 192 (216, 240) sts evenly spaced along edge of I-cord. Place marker (pm) and join for working in rnds, being careful not to twist sts. Knit 5 rnds. Work Rows 1–11 of Baubles chart. Change to MC and work even in St st until piece measures 7½ (9½, 11½)" (19 [24, 29] cm) from lower edge of I-cord. Work Rows 1–16 of Numbers chart, rep numeral sequence as needed to fit your size. Work Rows 1–11 of Baubles chart, then work Rows 1–34 of Crows chart (see page 28; see Note), beg and end as indicated for your size. Work Rows 1–3 of Seeds chart—piece measures 17¼ (19¼, 21¼)" (44 [49, 54] cm) from lower edge of I-cord.

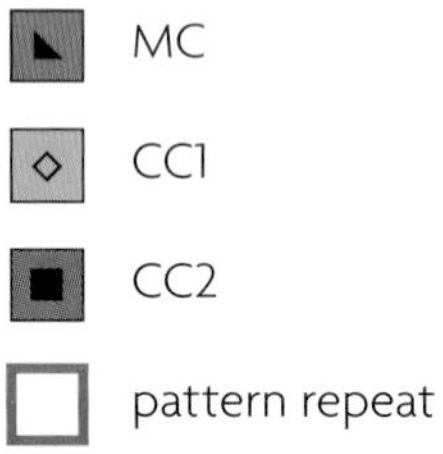

Baubles

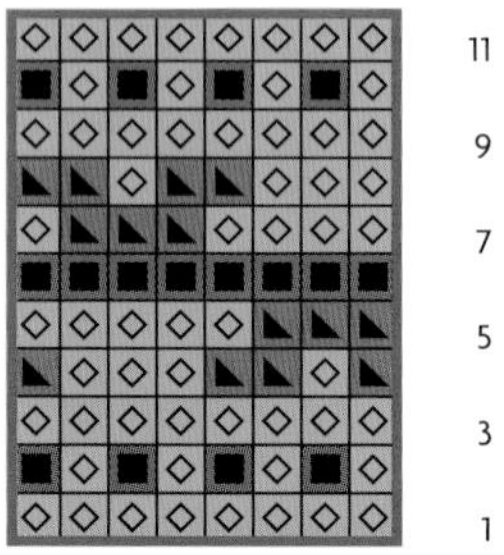

Seeds

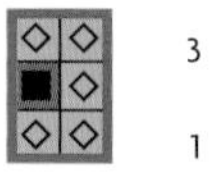

Numbers

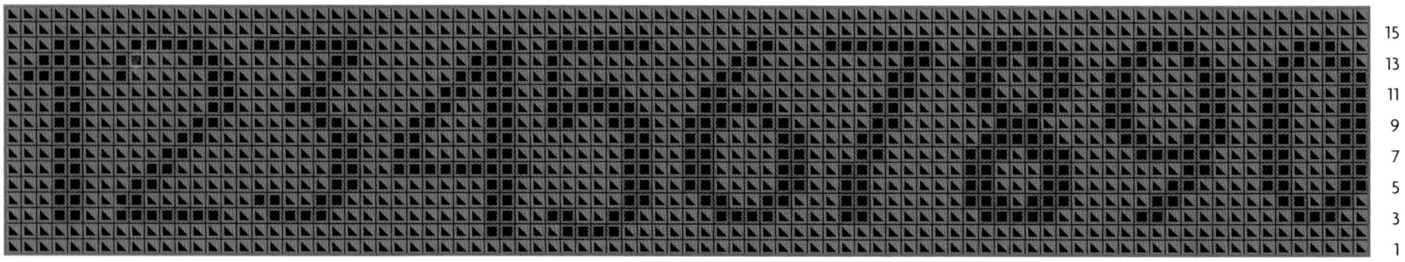

Place Stitches on Holders

With CC1, BO 3 sts for half of top of left armhole, k28 (32, 36) and place these sts on a holder for left front shoulder, k34 (38, 42) and place these sts on a second holder for front neck, k28 (32, 36) and place these sts on a third holder for right front shoulder, BO 6 sts for top of right armhole, k28 (32, 36) and place these sts on a fourth holder for right back shoulder, k34 (38, 42) and place these sts on a fifth holder for back neck, k28 (32, 36) and place these sts on a sixth holder for left back shoulder, BO rem 3 sts for other half of top of left armhole.

SLEEVES (make 2)

With CC1 and smaller dpn, CO 5 sts. Work 5-st I-cord until piece measures 8 (8¾, 9)" (20.5 [22, 23] cm) from CO. Place sts on holder. With larger dpn and MC, pick up and knit 48 (52, 54) sts evenly spaced along edge of I-cord. Pm and join for working in rnds, being careful not to twist sts. Knit 4 rnds. Inc 1 st each side of marker on next rnd, then every 5th rnd to beg of facing. *At the same time* work Rows 1–11 of Baubles chart, working inc'd sts

Crows

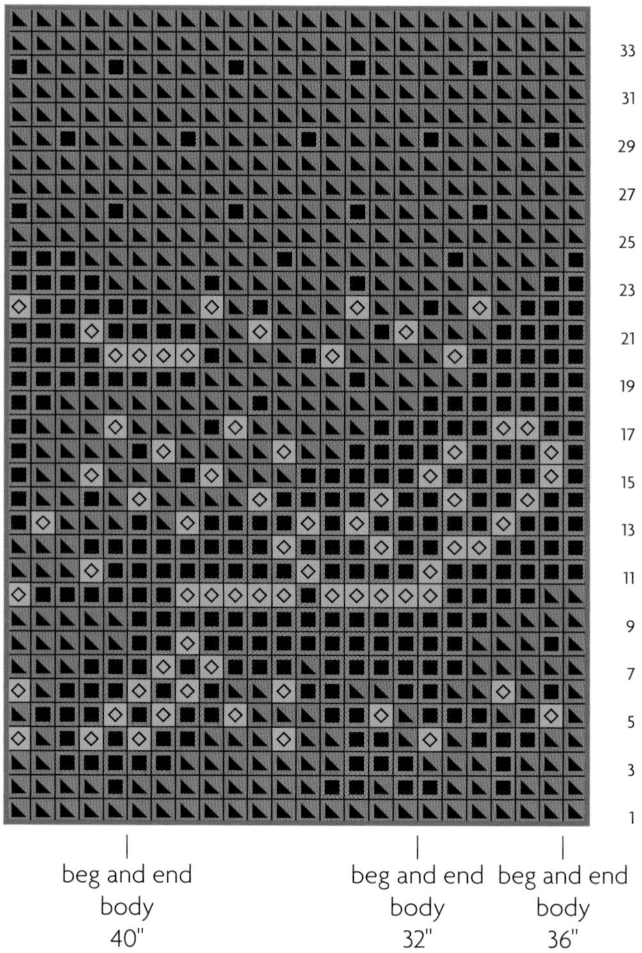

Note

There are three colors in Rows 4–22 of Crows chart. To work with just two colors per row, work the stitches designated as CC1 on these rows in the background color for that area, then use the duplicate stitch (see Glossary) to add the CC1 color after the knitting is complete.

- MC
- CC1
- CC2
- pattern repeat

into pattern. Change to MC and work in St st until piece measures 7 (9, 11)" (18 [23, 28] cm) from lower edge of I-cord. Work Rows 1–11 of Baubles chart. Work Rows 1–34 of Crows chart, then work Rows 29–34 again. Work Rows 1–3 of Seeds chart. With CC1, knit 1 rnd. Purl 6 rnds for facing, inc 1 st each side of marker every rnd. Loosely BO all sts.

FINISHING

Butt ends of I-cord tog and with CC1 threaded on a tapestry needle, sew tog as invisibly as possible. Weave in loose ends. Block pieces to measurements.

Cut Armholes and Neckline

Measure, mark, machine stitch, and cut armhole openings as described on pages 125–127. Measure, mark, machine stitch, and cut front neckline curve to a depth of 1½ (2, 2)" (3.8 [5, 5] cm), as described on page 129.

Seams

Place 28 (32, 36) held right front shoulder sts on one needle and corresponding right back shoulder sts on another needle. With RS tog, use the three-needle method as described on page 130 to BO the sts tog. With CC2, smaller needle, and RS facing, p28 (32, 36) held sts on left front shoulder edge for turning ridge. Work 6 rows even in St st for facing. BO all sts. Turn facing to WS and, with sharp-point sewing needle and matching thread, sew in place. With CC2, smaller needle, and RS facing, k28 (32, 36) held sts on left back shoulder edge. Work 5 rows even in St st for placket. Purl 1 row for turning ridge. Work 6 rows even in St st for facing. BO all sts. Turn facing to WS and sew in place.

Neck Edging

With MC, smaller cir needle, and RS facing, pick up and knit 36 (40, 44) sts evenly spaced along front neck edge, k34 (38, 42) held back neck sts, then pick up and knit 4 sts along shoulder placket—74 (82, 90) sts total. Beg and end with p2, work in k2, p2 rib for 7 rows. Purl 1 row for a turning ridge, then work 7 more rows in established rib for facing. Loosely BO all sts in patt. Turn facing to WS along turning ridge and sew in place.

Butt edges of top of left armhole and sew tog at armhole edge. Sew buttons to left back shoulder placket, the first at the armhole edge, the last on the neck edging, and the others evenly spaced in between. Make 5 button loops on left front shoulder edge opposite buttons as foll: Join CC2 to shoulder. Make a loop of CC2 large enough to accommodate button; take a st in shoulder to secure. Work buttonhole st (see Glossary) over loop to strengthen. Rep for rem buttons. Insert sleeves into armholes and sew in place as described on page 132.

“It was from Handel that I learned that style consists in force of assertion.”
—George Bernard Shaw

Some of the high points of the Baroque period include the invention of the pressure cooker, the popularity of the fork, and the fall from fashion of corsets (at least until the Victorians rediscovered them). No wonder, then, that Peter Paul Rubens's subjects were so voluptuous. Those who could afford to were eating and darned proud of it. Why not celebrate that spirit and take this pretty tote to market? Pick up some wine and a decadent dessert, too, while you're at it. You have my enthusiastic permission to embrace everything good: Go for Baroque.

go for baroque

FINISHED SIZE
About 14½" (37 cm) wide, 12½" (31.5 cm) high, and 4" (10 cm) deep, after felting.

YARN
Worsted weight (#4 Medium).
Shown Here: Lion Brand Lion Wool (100% wool; 158 yd [144 m]/85 g): #820-140 rose (MC) and #820-132 lemongrass (CC1), 2 balls each; #820-113 scarlet (CC2), 1 ball.

NEEDLES
Size U.S. 10½ (6.5 mm): 24" (60 cm) circular (cir). Adjust needle size if necessary to obtain the correct gauge.

NOTIONS
Marker (m); tapestry needle; sharp-point sewing needle and matching thread; two ¾" (2 cm) leather straps measuring 20" (51 cm) long (available from Homestead Heirlooms); piece of cardboard or plastic reinforcement measuring 3½" × 13" (9 × 33 cm) for bottom of bag; piece of fabric measuring 8" × 14" (20.5 × 35.5 cm) to cover reinforcement.

GAUGE
16 stitches and 20 rounds = 4" (10 cm) in charted pattern worked in rounds, before felting.

Baroque

+ MC

◿ CC1

pattern repeat

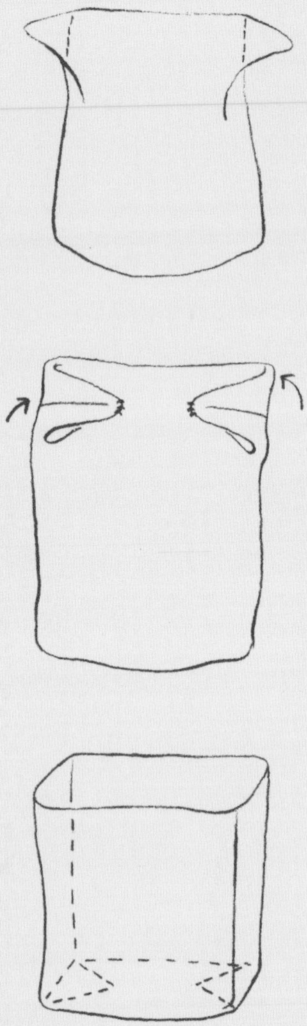

Stitch across corners, then fold corners to center to form gussets in base of bag.

TOTE

With CC2, CO 152 sts. Place marker (pm) and join for working in rnds, being careful not to twist sts. Work even in St st for 20 rnds. Change to CC1 and work 1 rnd even. Work Rows 1–42 of Baroque chart, then work Rows 1–23 again. Change to CC1 and knit 1 rnd even. Change to CC2 and knit 4 rnds even. **Picot rnd:** *K2tog, yo; rep from *. Knit 4 rnds even for facing. Loosely BO all sts.

FINISHING

Turn facing to WS along picot row and, with sewing needle and matching thread, sew in place. Sew bottom seam.

Large Flower (make 2 each in MC and CC2)

Using the backward-loop method (see Glossary), CO 80 sts. Do not join. Work 2 rows even in St st. **Dec row:** (RS) *K2tog; rep from *—40 sts rem. Work 1 row even in St st, then work dec row once more—20 sts rem. Work 1 row even in St st. BO all sts.

Medium Flower (make 2 each in MC and CC2)

Using the backward-loop method, CO 60 sts. Do not join. Work 2 rows even in St st. **Dec row:** (RS) *K2tog; rep from *—30 sts rem. Work 1 row even in St st, then work dec row once more—15 sts rem. Work 1 row even in St st. BO all sts.

Leaves (make 4)

With CC1, CO 3 sts. Work in St st, inc 1 st each end of needle every RS row 4 times—11 sts. Work 6 rows even. Dec 1 st at beg of next 10 rows—1 st rem. Cut yarn and pull tail through last st to secure.

Felting

Weave in loose ends. Felt bag, flowers, and leaves in washing machine using hot water wash, cold rinse, and lowest water level. Use a small amount of detergent to aid in felting. Check pieces every five minutes and remove when desired level of felting is reached. Pull pieces into shape and lay flat to dry.

Assembly

Coil flowers into shape and with sharp-point sewing needle and matching thread, stitch to secure. Turn bag inside out and stitch a 3½" (9 cm) long seam diagonally 1½" (3.8 cm) from lower corners to form gussets as shown at left. Turn right side out. Fold fabric in half lengthwise. Using a ½" (1.3 cm) seam allowance, sew side and bottom seam. Turn fabric bag RS out and insert cardboard. Sew final seam. Insert covered reinforcement into base of bag. Sew straps in place according to manufacturer's directions. (I secured the end of each strap with two buttons on the inside of bag.) Sew flowers and leaves over ends of straps, as shown in photo.

"Mary Mary Quite Contrary
How does your garden grow?
With silver bells and cockleshells
And pretty maids all in a row."
—Nursery Rhyme

queen of scots

FINISHED SIZE
About 38½ (41, 44½)" (98 [104, 113] cm) chest circumference, including 2 (2½, 2½)" (5 [6.5, 6.5] cm) front overlap. Sweater shown measures 38½" (98 cm).

YARN
Fingering weight (#1 Super Fine).
Shown here: Jamieson's Shetland Spindrift (100% wool; 115 yd [105 m]/25 g): #620 lilac (MC), 5 (6, 7) balls; #165 dusk (CC1), 3 (4, 4) balls; #147 moss (CC2), 2 (3, 3) balls; #615 hyacinth (CC3), 1 (2, 2) ball(s); #1300 aubretia (CC4), #239 purple heather (CC5), and #1190 burnt umber (CC6), 1 ball each for all sizes.

NEEDLES
Body: size U.S. 3 (3.25 mm): 24" (60 cm) circular (cir).
Binding: size U.S. 2 (2.75 mm): 24" (60 cm) cir. Adjust needle size if necessary to obtain the correct gauge.

NOTIONS
Stitch holders or waste yarn; markers (m); tapestry needle; sharp-point sewing needle and matching thread; five ⅞" (2.2 cm) buttons; 1 snap fastener.

GAUGE
30 stitches and 32 rounds = 4" (10 cm) in charted pattern on larger needle, worked in rounds.

Luckenbooths, named after the locked booths from which they were sold in Edinburgh, are charms or brooches that are exchanged as love tokens. Mary Queen of Scots is said to have received one at her engagement to Lord Darnley. My eldest brother visited Scotland when I was a child, and he sent me a replica of her luckenbooth, which I still wear today. It was sewn to the inside of my wedding gown for luck, and later, my babies wore it pinned to their shawls for health. The charm has become both talisman and trademark to me; so much a part of my identity that it had to be included in my collection. This is how I give you my luckenbooth, and with it my wishes for peace, love, and joy.

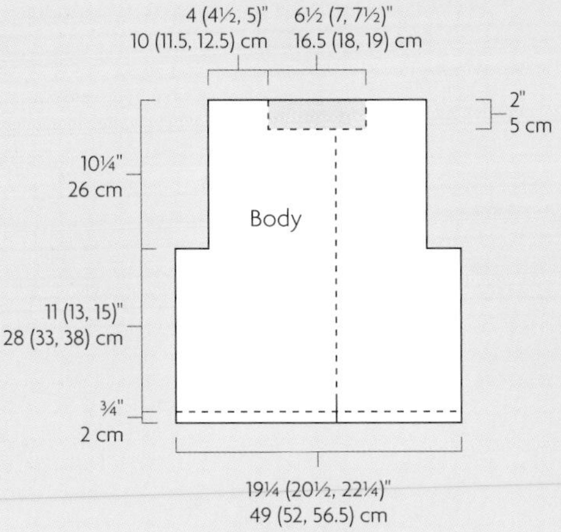

Thistle

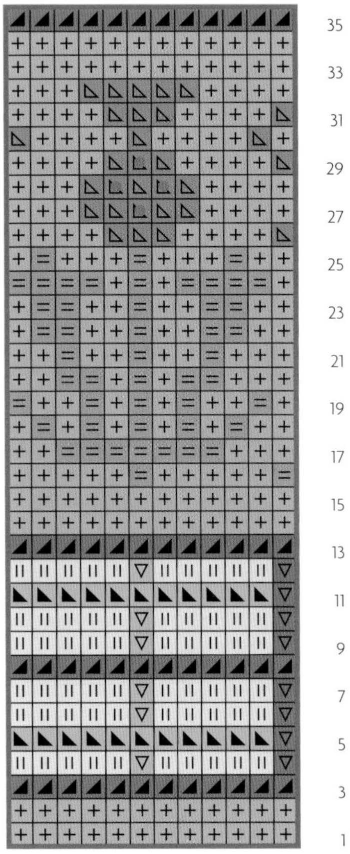

Tartan

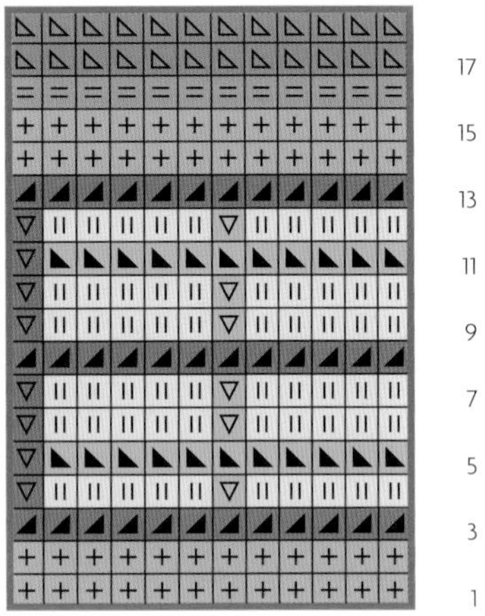

- MC
- CC1
- CC2
- CC3
- CC4
- CC5
- CC6
- knit with MC or CC6; duplicate st with CC5
- knit with MC; duplicate st with CC6
- CC1 French knot
- pattern repeat

Luckenbooth

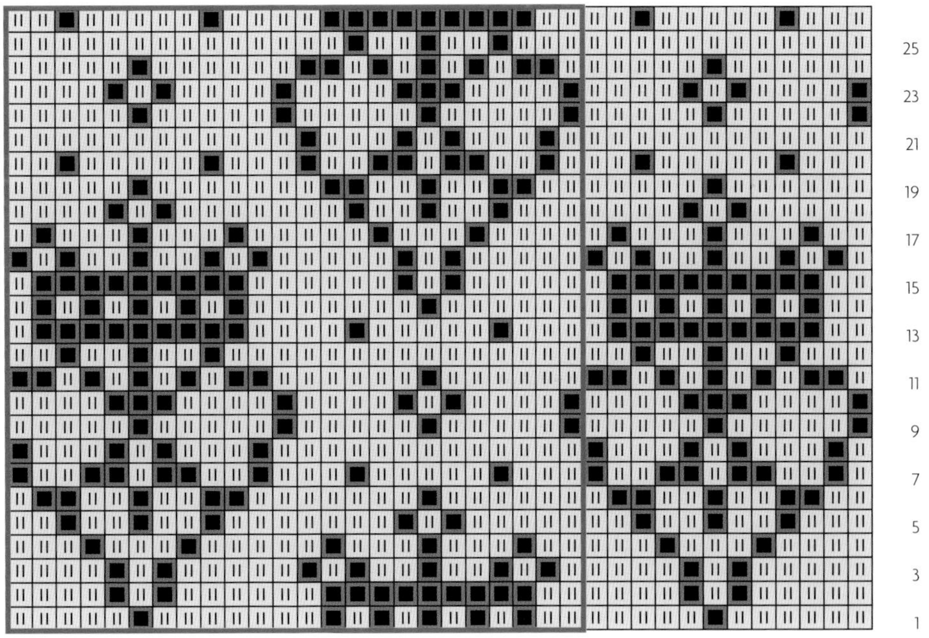

BODY

With CC2 and smaller cir needle, CO 300 (324, 348) sts. Work back and forth in St st for 5 rows. Knit 1 WS row for turning ridge. Change to larger cir needle and work 5 rows in St st. **Joining rnd:** Place marker (pm), use the backward-loop method (see Glossary) to CO 6 center front steek sts (see page 124; these sts are not included in st counts unless otherwise indicated), pm, join for working in rnds, being careful not to twist sts, and knit to end of rnd. Work Rows 1–35 of Thistle chart. Rep Rows 1–26 of Luckenbooth chart until piece measures 11 (13, 15)" (28 [33, 38] cm) from turning ridge.

Shape Armholes

Keeping in patt, k72 (82, 90) for right front, k36 and place these sts on holder or waste yarn for armhole, k108 (118, 130) for back, k36 and place these sts on holder for other armhole, k48 (52, 56) for left front. **Next rnd:** Work to right armhole, pm, use the backward-loop method to CO 6 right armhole steek sts (these sts are not included in st counts unless otherwise indicated), pm, work to left armhole, pm, CO 6 sts as before for left armhole steek, pm, work to end of rnd. Work even in patt until piece measures 19 (21, 23)" (48.5 [53.5, 58.5] cm) from turning ridge. Work Rows 1–18 of Tartan chart.

Place Stitches on Holders

With CC4 and beg at center of front steek, BO 3 steek sts, k42 (49, 53) and place these sts on a holder for right front neck, k30 (33, 37) and place these sts on a second holder for right front shoulder, BO 6 armhole steek sts, k30 (33, 37) and place these sts on a third holder for right back shoulder, k48 (52, 56) and place these sts on a fourth holder for back neck, k30 (33, 37) and place these sts on a fifth holder for left back shoulder, BO 6 armhole steek sts, k30 (33, 37) and place these sts on a sixth holder for left front shoulder, k18 (19, 19) and place these sts on a seventh holder for left front neck, BO rem 3 steek sts.

FINISHING

Work duplicate st and French knots (see Glossary for embroidery sts) as indicated on charts. Turn lower body facing to WS along turning ridge and, with sharp-point sewing needle and matching thread, sew in place invisibly. Weave in loose ends. Block to measurements.

Steeks

Mark, machine stitch, and cut center front and armhole steeks as described on pages 125–127. Measure, mark, machine stitch, and cut square front neckline to a depth of 2" (5 cm) as described on page 129.

Join Shoulders

Place 30 (33, 37) held right front shoulder sts on one needle and the corresponding 30 (33, 37) held right back shoulder sts on another needle. With RS tog, use the three-needle method as described on page 130 to BO the shoulder sts tog. Rep for other shoulder.

Neckline Binding

With CC2, smaller needle, RS facing, and beg at right front neck edge, pick up and knit 45 (52, 56) sts along straight edge of right front, pm, 15 sts along side of front neck to shoulder, pm, k48 (52, 56) held back neck sts, pm, pick up and knit 15 sts along side of left front neck, pm, and 21 (22, 22) sts along straight edge of left front neck—144 (156, 164) sts total. Work 6 rows back and forth in St st, dec 1 st each side of each m every RS row. Knit 1 WS row to form turning ridge. Work 6 rows in St st, inc 1 st each side of each m every RS row. BO all sts. Turn binding to WS along turning ridge and, with sharp-point sewing needle and matching thread, sew in place as invisibly as possible.

Front Binding

With CC2, smaller needle, and RS facing, pick up and knit 138 (154, 170) sts evenly spaced along right front edge between steek and body sts. Work 6 rows back and forth in St st. Knit 1 WS row for turning ridge. Work 6 rows in St st for facing. BO all sts. Turn binding to WS along turning ridge and sew in place. Rep for left front edge.

Armhole Binding

With CC2, smaller needle, and RS facing, k36 held right armhole sts, pm, pick up and knit 132 sts evenly spaced around armhole edge between steek and body sts, pm, and join for working in rnds—168 sts total. Knit 6 rnds, dec 1 st each side of each m every other rnd. Purl 1 rnd for turning ridge. Knit 6 rnds for facing, inc 1 st each side of each m every other rnd. BO all sts. Turn binding to WS along turning ridge and sew in place. Rep for left armhole.

Lay vest flat and overlap the front edges 2 (2½, 2½)" (5 [6.5, 6.5] cm) to determine button placement. Sew buttons to left front, placing the top button on the neckline binding, the bottom button 6½" (16.5 cm) below the top button, and the others evenly spaced in between. (**Note:** Heavy buttons may require reinforcement on WS for support.) Make button loops on right front edge opposite buttons as foll: Join CC2 to top of right front edge. Make a loop of yarn large enough to accommodate button; take a st in right front edge to secure. Work buttonhole st (see Glossary) over loop to strengthen. Rep for rem buttons. Sew snap fastener at neck edge to anchor left front underlap.

Splurge on yarn, closures, and trims you really love so your knitting will shout "Handmade!" instead of "Homemade."

"I do not want your pearls and jewels and fine clothes; but if you will love me, and let me live with you and eat from off your golden plate, and sleep on your bed, I will bring you your ball again..."
— *Grimm's Fairy Tales,* The Frog Prince

My sister and I have long referred to one another as "Frog" and "Toad." Probably due to early amphibian-based literature exposure, it's gone on so long we can't say for sure. Who is the frog and who is the toad has never been important and has changed according to whim. How fitting, then, that I would grow up to have a little boy who loves frogs. Before he could read, I made this pattern for my son as a love note. Mothers of non-reading children have likely been sending knitted messages to them in this way for as long as there have been sticks and string. Of course, my sister wants one now, too.

kiss that frog

FINISHED SIZE
25 (29, 33¼)" (63.5 [73.5, 84.5] cm) chest circumference. Sweater shown measures 25" (63.5 cm).

YARN
DK weight (#3 Light).
Shown here: Rauma Istra (100% wool; 111 yd [101 m]/ 50 g): #2078 moss green (MC) and #2034 army green (CC1), 2 (3, 3) balls each; #2037 charcoal gray heather (CC2), 2 balls for all sizes; #2027 dark rust red (CC3) and #2046 gold (CC4), 1 (2, 2) ball(s) each.

NEEDLES
Body: size U.S. 4 (3.5 mm): 24" (60 cm) circular (cir) and set of 4 or 5 double-pointed (dpn). *Facing:* size U.S. 2 (2.75 mm): 24" (60 cm) cir and set of 4 or 5 dpn. Adjust needle size if necessary to obtain the correct gauge.

NOTIONS
Stitch holders or waste yarn; markers (m); tapestry needle; sharp-point sewing needle and matching thread; 18" (45.5 cm) separating zipper; 1 yd (1 m) ⅞" (2.2 cm) bias tape or ribbon; 1" (2.5 cm) frog charm.

GAUGE
26 stitches and 28 rounds = 4" (10 cm) in charted pattern on larger needle, worked in rounds.

For a colorful surprise, knit the facings in coordinating or contrasting colors. Tell the recipient it's a secret code for "I love you."

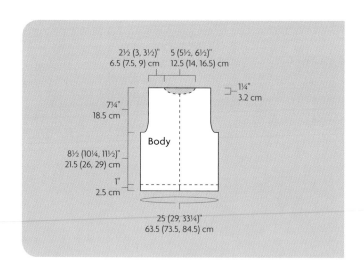

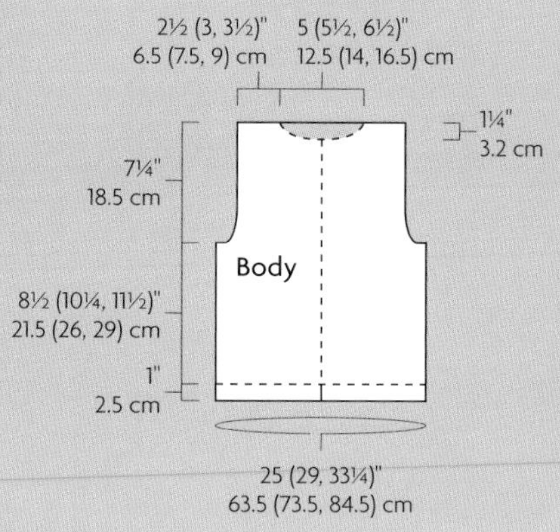

- × MC
- ◢ CC1
- ◇ CC2
- ■ CC3
- = CC4
- □ pattern repeat

Boxes

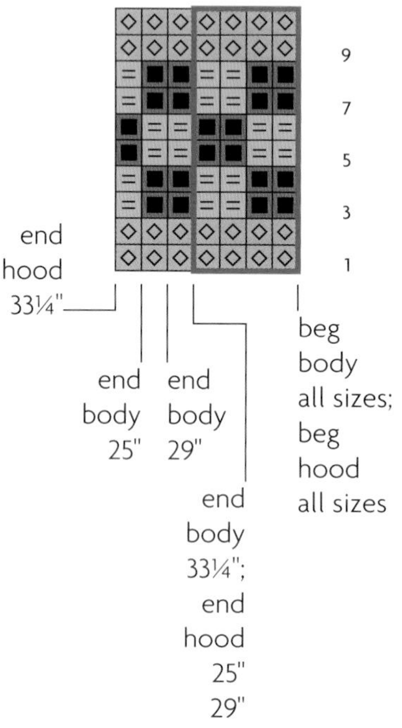

Stripes

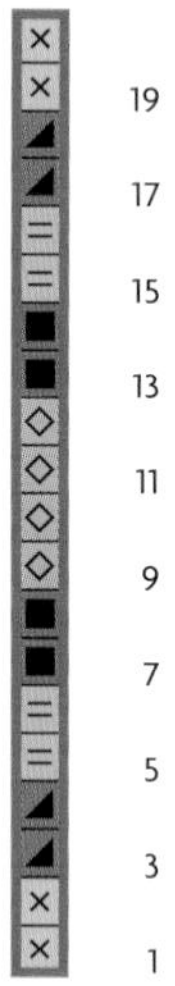

Frog

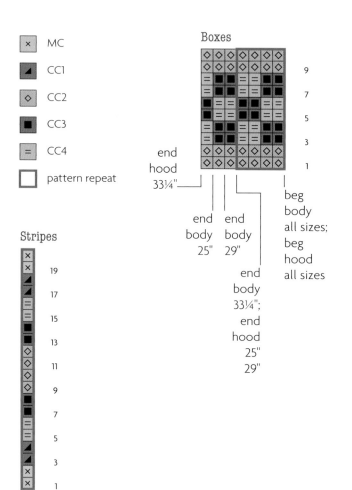

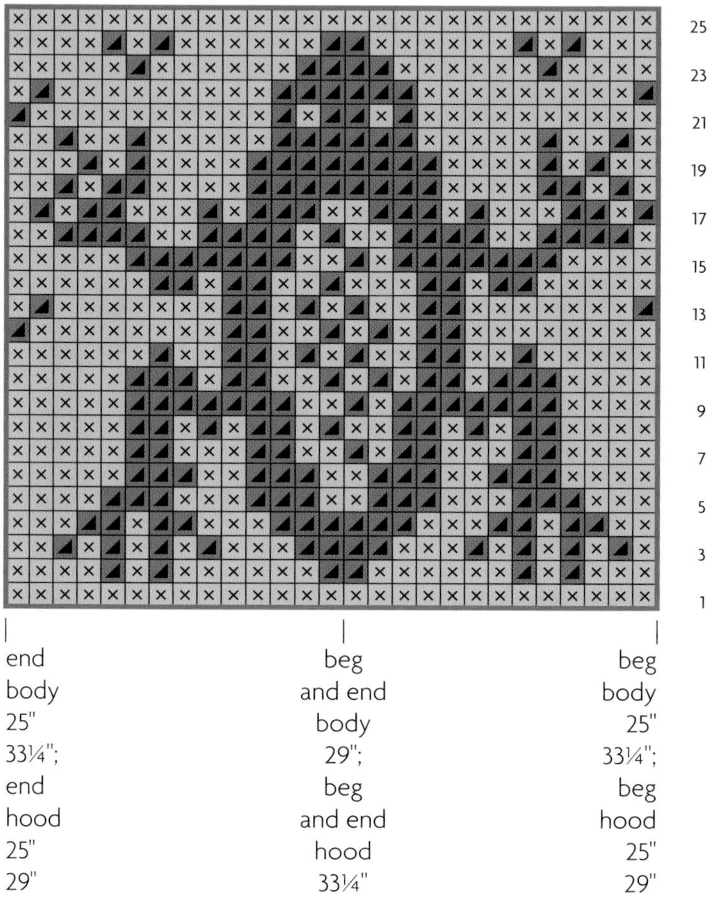

BODY

With CC2 and smaller cir needle, CO 162 (189, 216) sts. Do not join.

Hem

Work back and forth in St st for 6 rows. Change to CC3 and knit 2 rows (purl ridge is formed on RS). Change to CC2 and larger needle and work 5 more rows in St st. **Joining row:** Place marker (pm), use the backward-loop method (see Glossary) to CO 6 sts for front steek (see page 124; these sts are not included in st counts unless otherwise indicated), pm, join for working in rnds, being careful not to twist sts, and knit to end of rnd.

Cont for your size as foll:

size 25" (63.5 cm) only

Beg and ending as indicated for your size, work Rows 3–10 of Boxes chart, then work Rows 1–25 of Frog chart, then work Rows 1–10 of Boxes chart—piece measures 7" (18 cm) from turning ridge.

size 29" (73.5 cm) only

Work Rows 11–20 of Stripes chart, then, beg and ending as indicated for your size, work Rows 1–10 of Boxes chart, then work Rows 1–25 of Frog chart, then work Rows 1–10 of Boxes chart—piece measures 8¾" (22 cm) from turning ridge.

size 33¼" (84.5 cm) only

Work Rows 1–20 of Stripes chart, then, beg and ending as indicated for your size, work Rows 1–10 of Boxes chart, then work Rows 1–25 of Frog chart, then work Rows 1–10 of Boxes chart—piece measures 10¼" (26 cm) from turning ridge.

all sizes

Work Rows 1–10 of Stripes chart.

Shape Armholes

Cont with Rows 11–20 of Stripes chart, k34 (42, 49) for right front, BO 10 sts for right underarm, k74 (85, 98) for back, BO 10 sts for left underarm, k34 (42, 49) for left front—34 (42, 49) sts rem for each front, 74 (85, 98) sts rem for back. **Next rnd:** Knit to 4 sts before right armhole, k2tog, k2, pm, use the backward-loop method to CO 6 sts for right armhole steek, pm, k2, ssk, knit to 4 sts before left armhole, k2tog, k2, pm, use the backward-loop method to CO 6 sts for left armhole steek, pm, k2, ssk, knit to end of rnd—33 (41, 48) sts rem for each front, 72 (83, 96) sts rem for back. Knit 1 rnd. **Dec rnd:** *Knit to 4 sts before armhole m, k2tog,

k2, sl m, work steek sts, sl m, k2, ssk; rep from * once more, knit to end of rnd—4 sts dec'd. Rep the last 2 rnds 3 more times—29 (37, 44) sts rem for each front, 64 (75, 88) sts rem for back. Work Rows 1–10 of Boxes chart, then Rows 1–25 of Frog chart, keeping motifs centered on body as before (there will be partial motifs on each side of each armhole; see Centering Motifs on page 111), then Rows 1–5 of Boxes chart, ending last rnd at center of front steek.

Place Stitches on Holders

With CC4, BO 3 steek sts, k13 (17, 21) and place these sts on holder for right center front, k16 (20, 23) and place these sts on another holder for right front shoulder, BO 6 steek sts, k16 (20, 23) and place these sts on another holder for right back shoulder, k32 (35, 42) and place these sts on another holder for back neck, k16 (20, 23) and place these sts on another holder for left back shoulder, BO 6 steek sts, k16 (20, 23) and place these sts on another holder for left front shoulder, k13 (17, 21) and place these sts on another holder for left center front, BO rem 3 steek sts.

FINISHING

Weave in loose ends. Block to measurements.

Cut Steeks

Mark, machine stitch, and cut center front and armhole steeks as described on pages 125–127. Mark, machine stitch, and cut front neckline curve to a depth of 1¼" (3.2 cm) as described on page 129.

Place 16 (20, 23) held right front shoulder sts on one needle and corresponding 16 (20, 23) held right back shoulder sts on another needle. Hold the needles parallel with RS facing tog and use the three-needle method as described on page 130 to BO the shoulder sts tog. Rep for left shoulder.

Fold hem to WS along turning ridge and, with sharp-point sewing needle and matching thread, sew in place.

Hood

With CC2, larger cir needle, and RS facing, pick up and knit 3 sts along right front neck edge for steek, pm, pick up and knit 16 (19, 23) sts to back neck, k16 (17, 21) back neck sts from holder, pm, k16 (18, 21) back neck sts from holder, pick up and knit 16 (19, 23) sts to left front, pm, pick up and knit 3 sts for steek—64 (73, 88) sts total (hood steek sts are not included in st counts). Join for working in rnds. **Next rnd:** Knit, inc 22 (13, 25) sts evenly spaced—86 (86, 113) sts. Work Rows 1–20 of Stripes chart, then, beg and ending as indicated for your size, work Rows 1–10 of Boxes chart. *At the same time* shape hood as foll: **Inc rnd:** Knit to 2 sts before m, M1R (see Glossary), k2, sl m, k2 (3, 2), M1L (see Glossary), knit to end of rnd—2 sts inc'd. Knit 1 rnd. Rep the last 2 rnds 10 more times—108 (108, 135) sts. Beg and ending as indicated for your size, work Rows 1–25 of Frog chart, Rows 1–10 of Boxes chart, then Rows 1–10 of Stripes chart—piece measures about 10¾" (27.5 cm) from pick-up row. Place sts on holders or waste yarn.

Weave in loose ends. Block hood to measurements. Mark, machine stitch, and cut hood steek as described on pages 125–127. Place first 54 (54, 67) sts on one needle and rem 54 (54, 68) sts on another needle. With RS tog, use the three-needle method to BO sts tog, dec 0 (0, 1) st on second needle while working BO.

Front Binding

With CC2, larger cir needle, and RS facing, pick up and knit 137 (146, 152) sts evenly spaced from hem to top of hood between steek and body/hood sts, then 137 (146, 152) more sts from top of hood to opposite hem—274 (292, 304) sts total. Do not join. Work 6 rows in St st. Change to CC3 and work 1 row. Change to smaller cir needle and purl 1 RS row for turning ridge. Change to CC2 and work 6 more rows. Loosely BO all sts.

Armhole Binding

With CC2, larger dpn, and RS facing, pick up and knit 92 sts evenly spaced around armhole between steek and body sts. Pm and join for working in rnds. Knit 6 rnds. Change to CC3 and knit 1 rnd. Change to smaller dpn and purl 1 rnd for turning ridge. Change to CC2 and knit 6 more rnds. Loosely BO all sts. Repeat for other armhole. Fold bindings to WS along turning ridges and with sharp-point sewing needle and matching thread, sew in place.

Sew zipper (see Glossary) to front opening, trimming zipper to fit if necessary. Clip frog charm onto zipper pull. Cover neck cut edges on inside of vest with bias tape as described on page 132. Make a 3½" (9 cm) twisted cord tassel as foll: With 2 strands of yarn held tog, make two 7" (18 cm) twisted cords (see Glossary) with each of MC, CC2, CC3, and CC4 (8 cords total), and 3 twisted cords with CC1. Set aside one CC1 cord for finishing. Using a doubled strand of CC2, tie rem 10 cords tog at center. Fold bundle of cords in half. Tie reserved CC1 cord around bundle about 1" (2.5 cm) from fold to form neck of tassel. Sew tassel to point of hood.

"The teeth of the hound / Can sometimes be found / Due south of the Mailman's left knee. / His great postal feats / Include bringing treats / To fierce brave wee guard dogs like me."
—Crownridge Paisely Padpaw

The Scottish Terrier who owns my family takes her responsibilities very seriously. There are two children, two adults, and three cats in our home, all of whom require her vigilant supervision. Add to that the constant threat of Bad Guys (invisible ne'er-do-wells who can only be sensed by guard dogs and who must be barked at with high volume), and you can imagine the pressure that Paisley is under. Why, just getting adequate beauty sleep can be a challenge for her. Fortunately, our dog is an excellent multitasker. Just the other day, she managed to bark at the Bad Guys while taking a nap. The rest of us should be so highly skilled.

houndstooth

FINISHED SIZE

About 34½ (37, 39¼)" (87.5 [94, 99.5] cm) chest circumference. Sweater shown measures 37" (94 cm).

YARN

DK weight (#3 Light).

Shown here: Classic Elite Classic One-Fifty (100% wool; 150 yd [137 m]/50 g): #7213 black (MC), 7 (7, 8) balls; #7202 daisy (white; CC1), 4 (4, 5) balls; #7203 pewter (CC2), 2 balls for all sizes; #7258 radish (red; CC3), 1 ball for all sizes.

NEEDLES

Body and sleeves: size U.S. 6 (4 mm): 24" (60 cm) circular (cir) and set of 4 or 5 double-pointed (dpn).

Hem facing: size U.S. 4 (3.5 mm): 24" (60 cm) cir and set of 4 or 5 dpn. Adjust needle size if necessary to obtain the correct gauge.

NOTIONS

Stitch holders or waste yarn; markers (m); tapestry needle; sharp-point sewing needle and matching thread; two ¾" (2 cm) kilt straps (optional); ½ yd (45.5 cm) bias tape or ribbon.

GAUGE

26 stitches and 28 rounds = 4" (10 cm) in charted pattern on larger needle, worked in rounds.

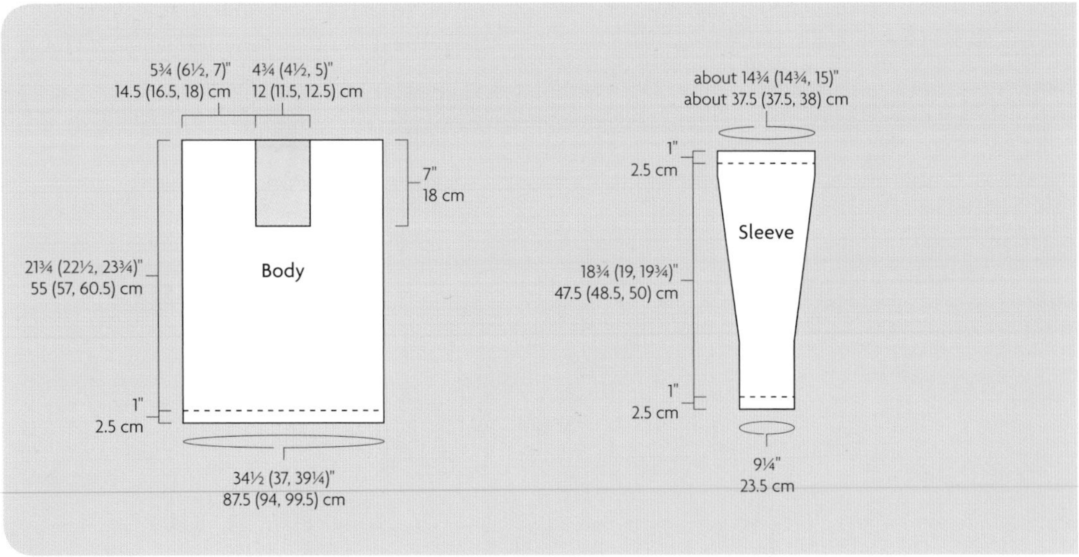

BODY

With MC and smaller cir needle, CO 225 (240, 255) sts. Place marker (pm) and join for working in rnds, being careful not to twist sts. Knit 6 rnds. Purl 1 rnd for turning ridge. Change to larger cir needle and knit 6 rnds. Work Rows 1–28 of Terrier chart. With MC, knit 1 rnd. Rep Rows 1–5 of Houndstooth chart until piece measures 14¾ (15½, 16¾)" (37.5 [39.5, 42.5] cm) from turning ridge.

Shape Neck

Cont in patt, k41 (45, 48), BO 30 sts for front neck, knit to end of rnd—195 (210, 225) sts rem. **Next rnd:** K41 (45, 48), pm, use the backward-loop method (see Glossary) to CO 6 steek sts (see page 124; these sts are not included in st counts unless otherwise indicated), pm, knit to end of rnd. Work even in patt until piece measures about 20¾ (21½, 22¾)" (52.5 [54.5, 58] cm) from turning ridge, ending with chart Row 5. Work Rows 1–6 of Stripes chart.

Place Stitches on Holders

With MC, BO 3 sts for half of top of left armhole, k38 (42, 45) and place these sts on holder for left front shoulder, BO 6 center front steek sts, k38 (42, 45) and place these sts on another holder for right front shoulder, BO 6 sts for top of right armhole, k38 (42, 45) and place these sts on another holder for right back shoulder, k31 (30, 33) and place these sts on another holder for back neck, k38 (42, 45) and place these sts on another holder for left back shoulder, BO last 3 sts for other half of top of left armhole.

- ■ MC
- – CC1
- × CC2
- ◣ CC3
- ▽ knit with MC or CC2; duplicate st with CC3
- □ pattern repeat

Terrier

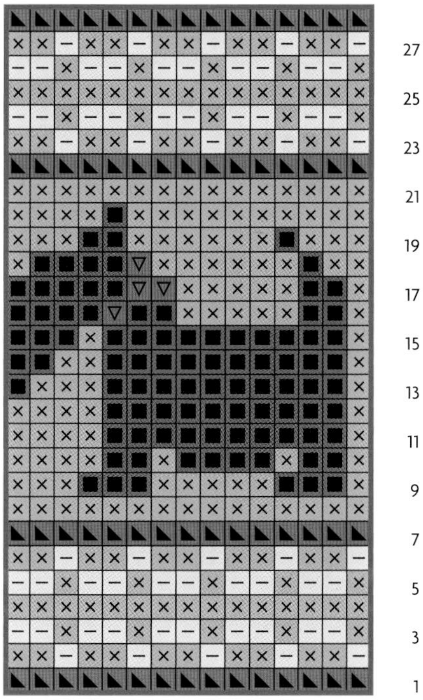

Houndstooth

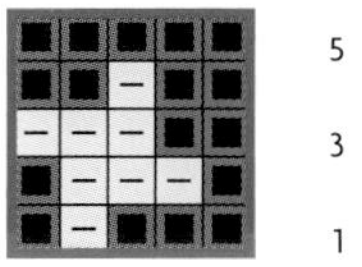

Stripes

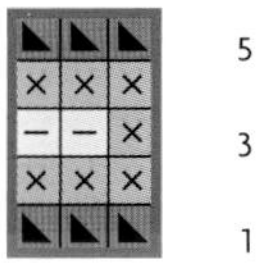

SLEEVES

With MC and smaller dpn, CO 60 sts. Pm and join for working in rnds, being careful not to twist sts. Knit 6 rnds. Purl 1 rnd for turning ridge. Change to larger dpn. Knit 6 rnds. Work Rows 1–28 of Terrier chart. With MC, knit 1 rnd, inc 1 st at beg and end of rnd—62 sts. Rep Rows 1–5 of Houndstooth chart, inc 1 st each side of marker every 5th rnd, working new sts into patt, until piece measures 17¾ (18, 18¾)" (45 [45.5, 47.5] cm) from turning ridge, ending with Row 5 of chart. Work Rows 1–6 of Stripes chart. With MC, knit 1 rnd. Purl 6 rnds for facing, inc 1 st each side of marker every rnd. Loosely BO all sts.

FINISHING

Weave in loose ends. Turn hems to WS and sew in place with sewing thread and sharp-point needle. Block pieces to measurements.

Steeks

Machine stitch and cut center front steek and armhole openings as described on pages 125–127.

With RS tog, use the three-needle method as described on page 130 to BO the shoulder sts tog.

Collar

With MC, smaller needle, RS facing, and beg at lower edge of neck opening, pick up and knit 53 sts along side of right front neck edge between steek and body sts, k31 (30, 33) held back neck sts, then pick up and knit 53 sts along side of left front neck edge between steek and body sts—137 (136, 139) sts total. Working back and forth in rows, work in k1, p1 rib until piece measures 2½" (6.5 cm) from pick-up row, ending with a WS row. Using the tubular 1×1 rib method (see Glossary), BO all sts. Align collar selvedge edges with BO neck edge. With MC threaded on a tapestry needle, sew collar selvedge edges to WS of BO neck edge. Cover steek edges on inside of collar with bias tape or ribbon as described on page 132.

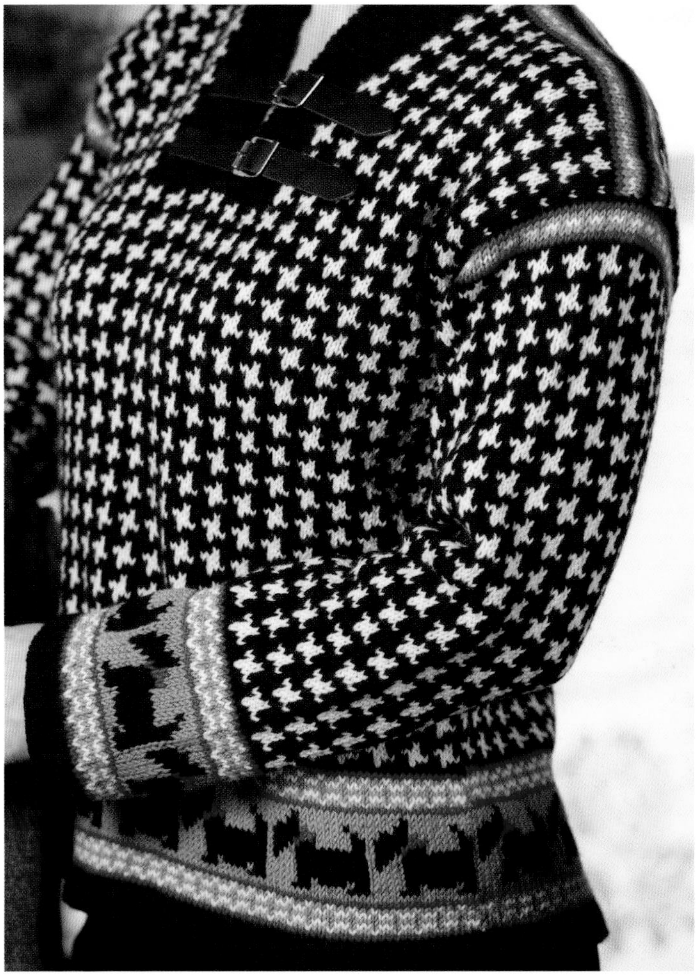

Join Sleeves

Insert sleeves into body and sew in place as described on page 132. Fold sleeve facings to WS to cover cut edges of openings and, with sharp-point sewing needle and matching thread, sew in place.

Sew one kilt strap to right front collar at pick-up row, ½" (1.3 cm) above lower edge of collar. Sew second strap ¾" (2 cm) above first. Sew buckles to left front collar at pick-up row opposite straps.

With CC3 threaded on a tapestry needle, work duplicate st (see Glossary) to add dog collars to body and sleeves as indicated on Terrier chart.

"Remarkable bird, the Norwegian Blue.
Beautiful plumage."
—Monty Python's Flying Circus

norwegian blue

Although the Scandinavian method of stranded color knitting is often referred to as "Norwegian," there are no traditional Norse motifs in this book. This design is my version of a "Norwegian" sweater. It was inspired by a challenge issued to me by my husband: "I want a sweater called 'Norwegian Blue.'" He didn't give any other guidelines, but I knew immediately that he was referring to his favorite comedy sketch of all time. I found the parrot motif in an old filet crochet chart. The inscription around the shoulders translates to "Pining for the Fjords."

FINISHED SIZE

43¾ (46¼, 48½)" (111 [117.5, 123] cm) chest circumference. Sweater shown measures 46¼" (117.5 cm).

YARN

Sportweight (#2 Fine).

Shown here: Harrisville Designs New England Shetland (100% wool; 217 yd [198 m]/50 g): #48 dove grey (MC), 6 balls for all sizes; #17 Bermuda blue (CC1) and #31 cobalt (CC2), 2 balls each for all sizes; #32 navy (CC3), 1 (1, 2) ball(s); #35 chianti (CC4), 1 ball for all sizes.

NEEDLES

Body and sleeves: size U.S. 3 (3.25 mm): 16" (40 cm) and 32" (80 cm) circular (cir). *Facings:* size U.S. 2 (2.75 mm): 32" (80 cm) cir. Adjust needle size if necessary to obtain the correct gauge.

NOTIONS

Stitch holders or waste yarn; markers (m); tapestry needle; sharp-point sewing needle and matching thread; seven 2½" (6.5 cm) pewter hooks; 1½ yd (1.4 m) of 1¼" (3.2 cm) bias tape or ribbon to cover sleeve seams; 1¾ yd (1.6 m) each of ¼" (6 mm) and ⅜" (1 cm) ribbon/braid trims (optional); 2¼ yd (2.1 m) of ½" (1.3 cm) ribbon/braid trim (optional).

GAUGE

26 stitches and 36 rounds = 4" (10 cm) in charted pattern on larger needle, worked in rounds.

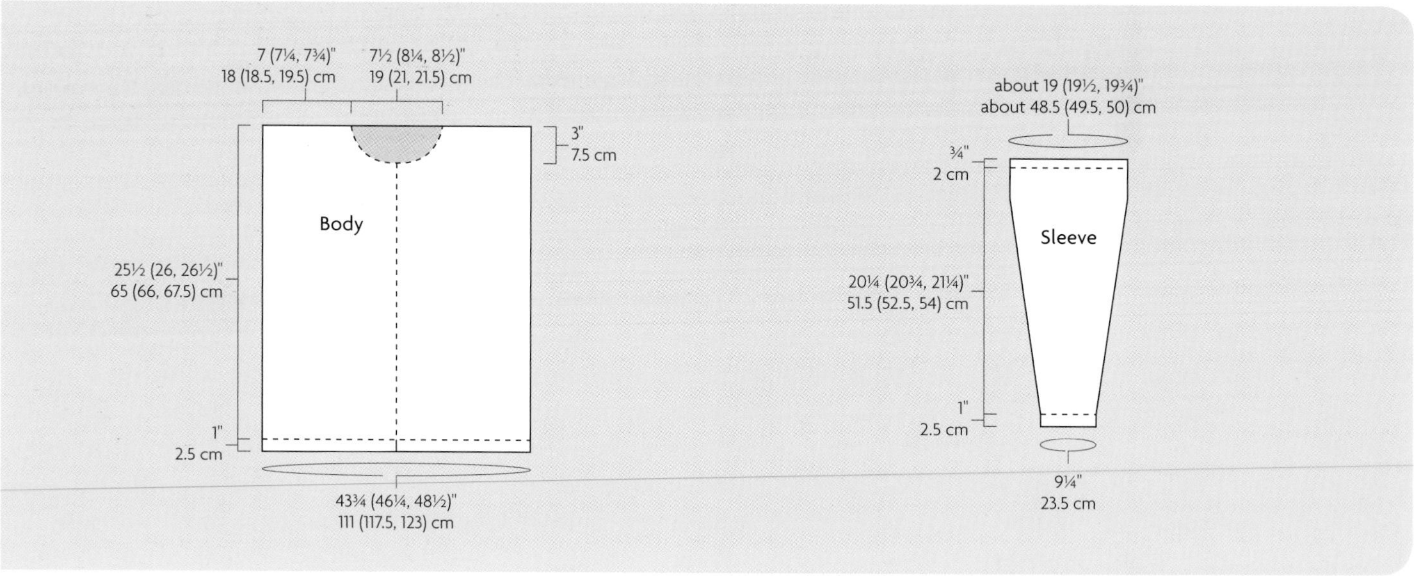

BODY

With CC2 and smaller cir needle, CO 285 (300, 315) sts. Do not join. Beg and ending with a WS row, work 9 rows in St st for facing. Purl 1 RS row for turning ridge. **Joining rnd:** Change to larger cir needle, place marker (pm), use the backward-loop method (see Glossary) to CO 6 sts for steek (see page 124; these sts are not included in st counts unless otherwise indicated), pm, join for working in rnds, being careful not to twist sts. Work Rows 1–9 of Hem chart. Work Rows 1–56 of Parrot chart. Rep Rows 1–18 of Body and Sleeve chart until piece measures 23 (23½, 24)" (58.5 [59.5, 61] cm) from turning ridge. Work Rows 1–21 of Verse chart, repeating patt rep as many times as possible, ending with an incomplete rep.

Place Stitches on Holders

With MC and beg at center of front steek, BO 3 steek sts, k22 (23, 24) and place these sts on holder for right center front, k45 (47, 50) and place these sts on another holder for right front shoulder, BO 6 sts for top of right armhole, k45 (47, 50) and place these sts on another holder for right back shoulder, k49 (54, 55) and place these sts on another holder for back neck, k45 (47, 50) and place these sts on another holder for left back shoulder, BO 6 sts for top of left armhole, k45 (47, 50) and place these sts on another holder for left front shoulder, k22 (23, 24) and place these sts on another holder for left center front, BO rem 3 steek sts.

SLEEVES

Note: Both sleeves are worked simultaneously as described on page 122.

Cuffs

With CC2 and smaller cir needle, CO 60 sts. Do not join. Work 9 rows in St st for facing. Knit 1 WS row for turning ridge. Change to larger cir needle and work Rows 1–9 of Hem chart. Cut off yarn. Place sts on holder. Make another cuff to match.

Join Cuffs

Change to MC. With RS facing, knit across 60 sts of first cuff, pm, use the backward-loop method to CO 6 sts for steek, knit across 60 sts of second cuff, pm, CO 6 more steek sts, pm, and join for working in rnds, being careful not to twist sts—60 sts for each sleeve; 6 steek sts between each sleeve. Rep Rows 1–18 of Body and Sleeve chart, inc 1 st at each end of each sleeve every 5th rnd (4 incs per inc rnd) and working new sts into patt until piece measures 18 (18½, 19)" (45.5 [47, 48.5] cm) from CO or desired length. Work Rows 1–21 of Verse chart, repeating patt rep as many times as possible, ending with an incomplete rep. **Next rnd:** With MC, knit first sleeve sts and place these sts on a holder or waste yarn, BO 6 steek sts, knit second sleeve sts and place these sts on a holder, BO rem 6 steek sts.

- MC
- CC1
- CC2
- CC3
- CC4
- pattern repeat

Hem

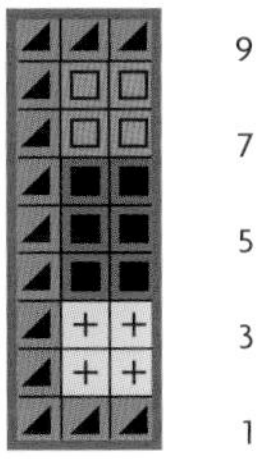

Parrot

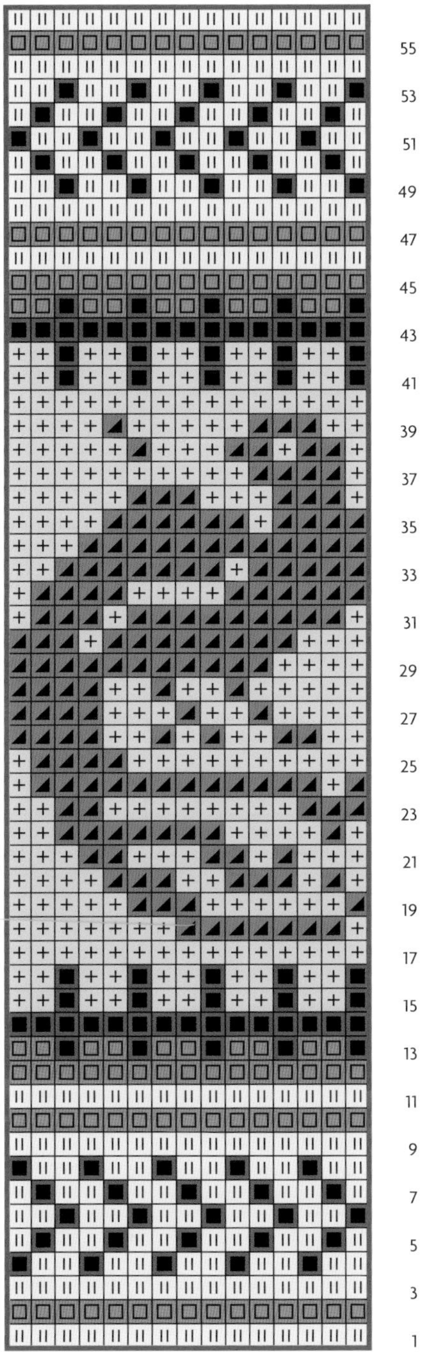

Body and Sleeve

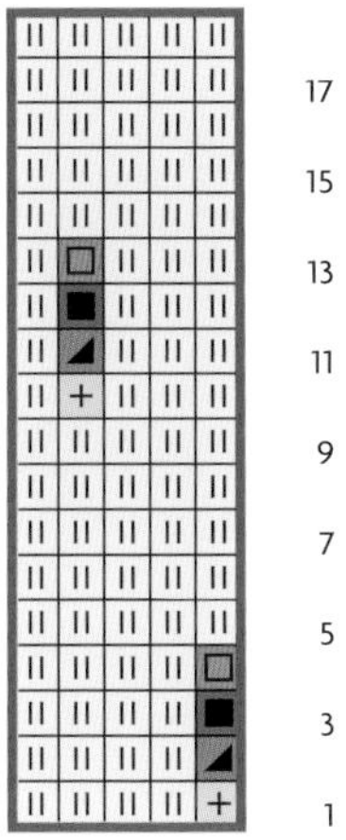

Verse

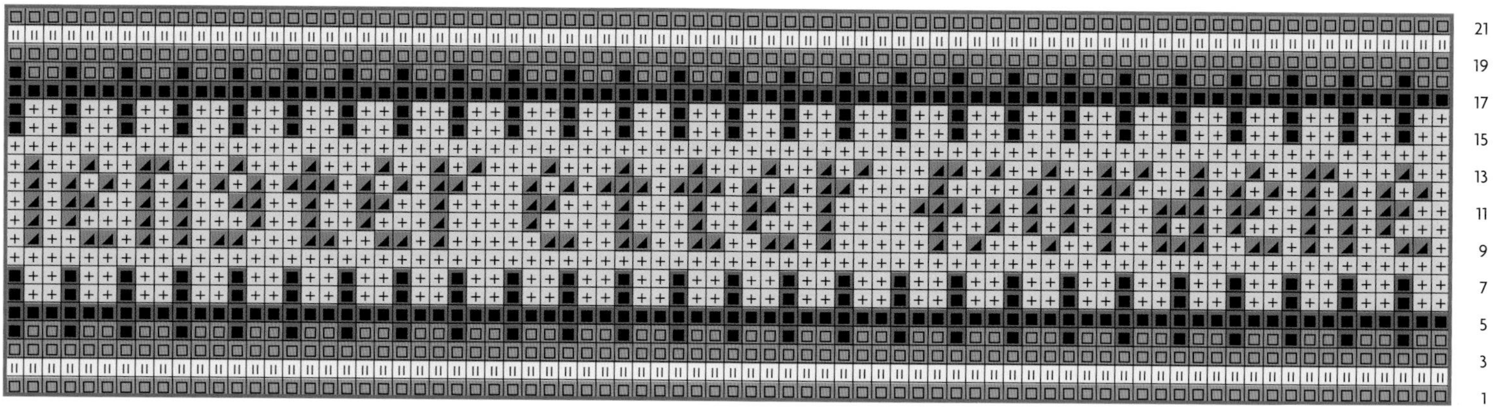

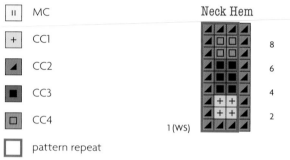

- MC
- CC1
- CC2
- CC3
- CC4
- pattern repeat

Neck Hem

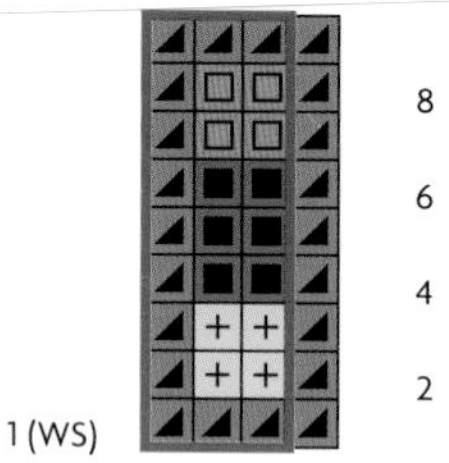

FINISHING

Weave in loose ends. Block pieces to measurements.

Cut Steeks, Armhole Openings, and Neckline

Mark, machine stitch, and cut center front steek and armhole openings as described on pages 125–127. Mark, machine stitch, and cut sleeve steeks to separate sleeves. Mark, machine stitch, and cut front neckline curve to a depth of 3" (7.5 cm) as described on page 129.

Place 45 (47, 50) held right front shoulder sts on one needle and corresponding 45 (47, 50) held right back shoulder sts on another needle. With RS tog, use the three-needle method as described on page 130 to BO the shoulder sts tog. Rep for other shoulder.

Turn facings to WS along turning ridge. With sharp-point sewing needle and matching thread, sew in place.

Sleeve Facings

With MC threaded on a tapestry needle, sew underarm sleeve seams. Return held sleeve sts to larger needle. Pm and join for working in rnds. With MC, purl 6 rnds for facing, inc 1 st each side of marker every rnd. Loosely BO all sts. Cover seam on inside of sleeve with 1¼" (3.2 cm) wide ribbon or bias tape as described on page 132.

Front Facing

With CC2, smaller cir needle, and RS facing, pick up and knit 150 (157, 164) sts evenly spaced along left front edge between steek and body sts. Do not join. Work 4 rows in St st. Knit 1 WS row for turning ridge. Work 5 more rows in St st for facing. Loosely BO all sts. Fold facing to WS along turning ridge and, with sharp-point sewing needle and matching thread, sew in place. Rep for right front edge.

Neck Facing

With CC2, smaller cir needle, and RS facing, pick up and knit 33 (35, 36) sts evenly spaced along right front neck edge, k49 (54, 55) held back neck sts, then pick up and knit 33 (35, 36) sts evenly spaced along left front neck edge—115 (124, 127) sts total. Do not join. Beg with a WS row and work Rows 1–9 of Neck Hem chart. With CC2, purl 1 RS row for turning ridge. Work 9 more rows in St st for facing. Loosely BO all sts. Fold facing to WS along turning ridge and, with sharp-point sewing needle and matching thread, sew in place.

Insert sleeves into armholes and sew in place, following directions on page 132. With sharp-point sewing needle and matching thread, sew sleeve facings in place.

Apply optional ribbon/braid trim along side of front bands, placing ¼" (6 mm) wide ribbon next to band, ½" (1.3 cm) wide ribbon next to ¼" (6 mm) ribbon, and ⅜" (1 cm) wide ribbon next to ½" (1.3 cm) ribbon. Apply optional ½" (1 cm) wide ribbon around neckline just below Neck Hem chart. Sew clasps to front, placing the highest on the pick-up rnd for the Neck Hem chart, the lowest just above the lower edge Hem chart, and the others evenly spaced in between.

"The day unfolds like a lotus bloom,
Pink at the tip and gold at the core,
Rising up swiftly through waters of gloom
That lave night's shore."

—Mary McNeil Fenollosa

lotus blossom

FINISHED SIZE

About 32 (34¼, 36½)" (81.5 [87, 92.5] cm) chest circumference. Vest shown measures 34¼" (87 cm).

YARN

Sportweight (#2 Fine)

Shown here: Louet Gems (100% superwash wool; 225 yd [206 m]/100 g): #47 terra cotta (MC1), 2 (2, 3) skeins; #04 soft coral (MC2), 2 skeins for all sizes; #58 burgundy (CC1), #11 cherry red (CC2), and #62 citrus orange (CC3), 1 skein each for all sizes.

NEEDLES

Body and sleeves: size U.S. 3 (3.25 mm): 24" (60 cm) circular (cir). *Hem facings:* size U.S. 2 (2.75 mm): 24" (60 cm) cir and set of 4 or 5 double-pointed (dpn). Adjust needle size if necessary to obtain the correct gauge.

NOTIONS

Markers (m); stitch holders or waste yarn; tapestry needle; sharp-point sewing needle and matching thread; six 1" (2.5 cm) bracelet toggles; 1 snap fastener.

GAUGE

28 stitches and 28 rounds = 4" (10 cm) in charted pattern on larger needle, worked in rounds.

Sometimes my designs become little more than vehicles for beautiful closures. That's like saying that I love hot fudge so much I'm forced to eat ice cream, but if the shoe fits. . . . I have actually been known to design extra openings in garments, purely as excuses for beautiful buttons and hooks. I often repurpose pretty things as sweater closures that began life with different intentions. Such is the case with the fittings for Lotus Blossom. When I fell in love with these bracelet toggles, I immediately set about to make a sweater that would show them off. I knew right away that an asymmetrical opening would suit them best, and the rest just seemed to fall into place.

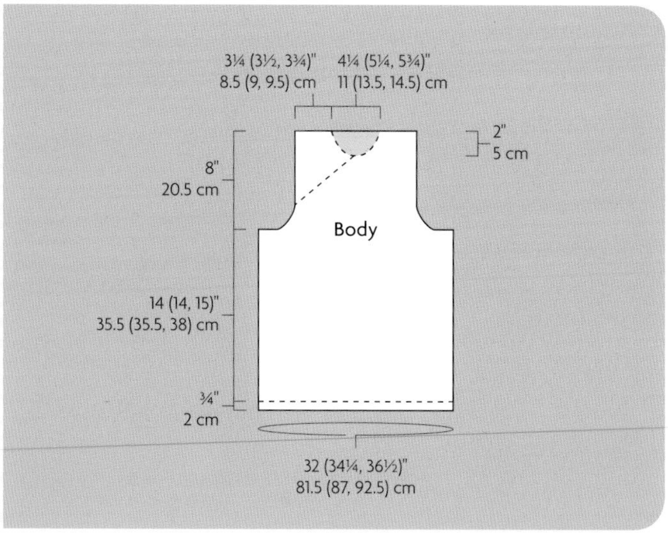

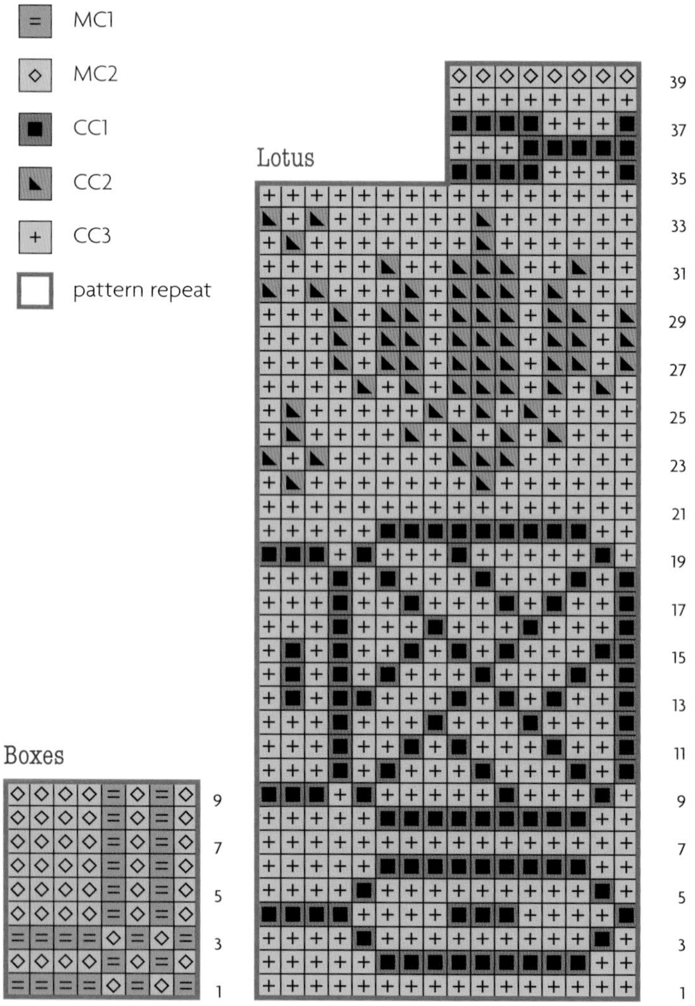

BODY

With MC1 and smaller cir needle, CO 224 (240, 256) sts. Place marker (pm) and join for working in rnds, being careful not to twist sts. Rnd begins at left side seam. Knit 5 rnds, then purl 1 rnd for turning ridge. Change to larger cir needle and knit 5 rnds. Change to CC2 and knit 1 rnd, placing additional marker after 112 (120, 128) sts to denote side "seam." Work Rows 1–39 of Lotus chart. Rep Rows 1–9 of Boxes chart until piece measures 14 (14, 15)" (35.5 [35.5, 38] cm) from turning ridge.

Shape Armholes

Place the last 12 sts worked onto a holder or waste yarn. Keeping in patt, work the next 12 sts and place these sts on the same holder (24 sts total on holder for armhole), work to m, place the last 12 sts worked onto another holder, work the next 12 sts and place these sts on the same holder (24 sts total on holder for armhole), work to end of rnd—176 (192, 208) sts rem; 88 (96, 104) sts each for front and back. **Next rnd:** Keeping in patt, work to armhole, pm, use the backward-loop method (see Glossary) to CO 6 steek sts (see page 124; steek sts are not included in st counts unless otherwise indicated), pm, work to other armhole, pm, CO 6 sts for steek, pm. **Dec rnd:** K2, ssk, work to 4 sts before m, k2tog, k2, work 6 steek sts, k2, ssk, work to last 4 sts, k2tog, k2, work 6 steek sts—4 sts dec'd. Work 1 rnd even. Rep the last 2 rnds 5 more times—152 (168, 184) sts rem. Work even until piece measures 22 (22, 23)" (56 [56, 58.5] cm) from turning ridge.

Place Stitches on Holders

With MC2, k23 (24, 26) and place these sts on a holder for left front shoulder, k30 (36, 40) and place these sts on a second holder for front neck, k23 (24, 26) and place these sts on a third holder for right front shoulder, BO 6 steek sts, k23 (24, 26) and place these sts on a fourth holder for right back shoulder, k30 (36, 40) and place these sts on a fifth holder for back neck, k23 (24, 26) and place these sts on a sixth holder for left back shoulder, BO rem 6 steek sts.

FINISHING

Weave in loose ends. Block to measurements.

Cut Armholes and Neckline

Machine stitch and cut armhole steeks as described on pages 125–127. Machine stitch and cut front neckline curve to a depth of 2" (5 cm) as described on page 129.

Collar

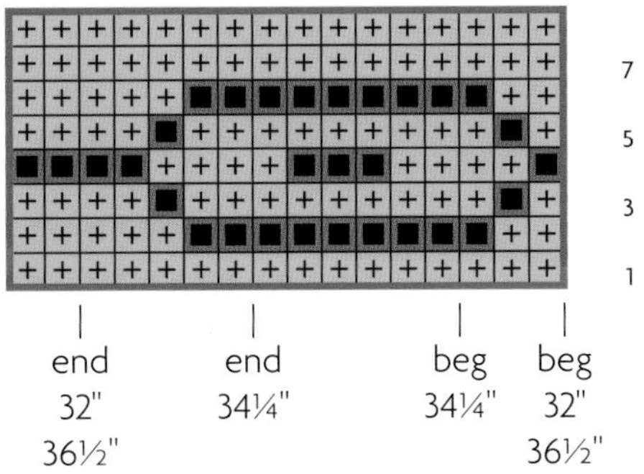

Join Shoulders

Place 23 (24, 26) left front shoulder sts on one needle, 23 (24, 26) left back shoulder sts on another needle, hold the needles parallel with RS tog, and use the three-needle method as described on page 130 to BO the sts tog. Rep for other shoulder.

Collar

With CC3, larger needle, RS facing, and beg at center front neck, pick up and knit 3 sts for steek, pm, pick up and knit 16 (17, 19) sts along right front neck edge, k30 (36, 40) held back neck sts, pick up and knit 16 (17, 19) sts along left front neck edge, pm, pick up and knit 3 sts for steek—62 (70, 78) sts total for collar and 6 steek

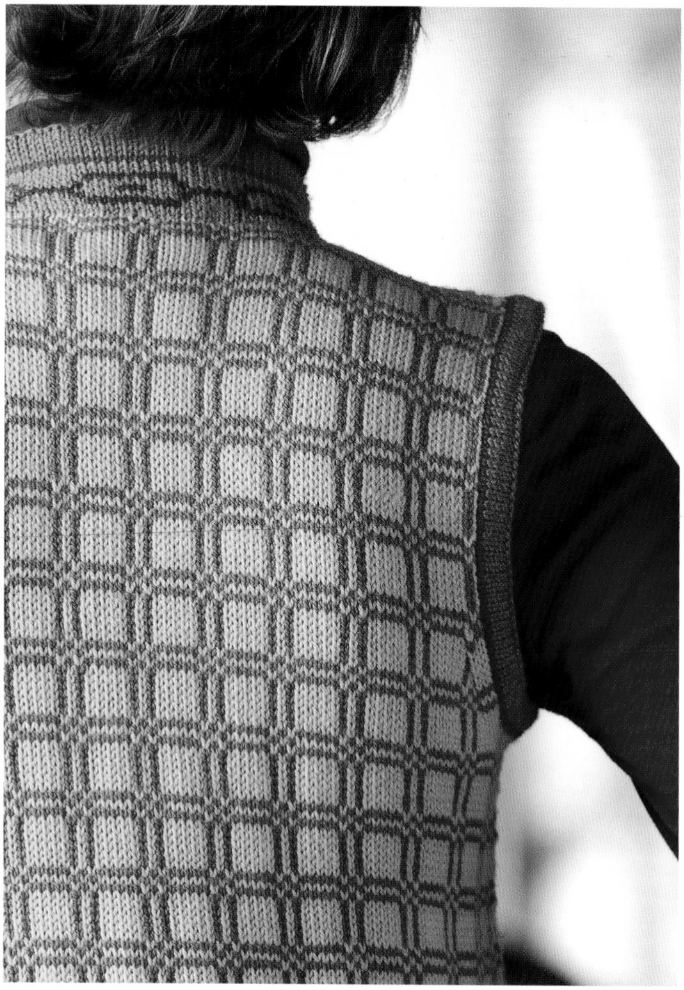

Be on the lookout for interesting findings that will enhance or replace traditional closures. Beads, smooth metal scraps, shells, driftwood, knotted cords, and polymer clay shapes are all interesting possibilities. Fabric-covered buttons and invisible closures such as hooks-and-eyes and snaps can also make good choices.

sts. Beg and end as indicated for your size, work Rows 1–8 of Collar chart. Change to CC2 and knit 1 rnd. Change to MC1 and knit 5 rnds, purl 1 rnd for turning ridge. **Next rnd:** BO 6 steek sts. Work back and forth in k1, p1 rib for 1½" (3.8 cm) from turning ridge for facing. Loosely BO all sts.

Beg at top of collar steek, mark a straight line to base of collar. Mark a diagonal line from this point to another point 6" (15 cm) down right armhole from shoulder seam, as shown on schematic on page 60. Machine stitch and cut opening as before.

Neck Bindings

upper diagonal edge

With MC1, smaller needle, RS facing, and beg at armhole, pick up and knit 32 (38, 48) sts evenly spaced along upper diagonal edge. Beg with a WS row, work 6 rows in St st. Knit 1 WS row for turning ridge, then work 8 more rows in St st. Loosely BO all sts.

right collar

With CC2, smaller needle, RS facing, and beg at lower collar edge, pick up and knit 15 sts along right collar edge between steek and collar sts. Purl 1 WS row. Change to MC1 and work 5 rows in St st, inc 1 st at beg of every RS row—18 sts. Knit 1 WS row for turning ridge. Work 8 rows even in St st. Loosely BO all sts.

left collar

With CC2, smaller needle, RS facing, and beg at upper collar edge, pick up and knit 15 sts along left collar edge between steek and collar sts. Purl 1 WS row. Change to MC1 and work 5 rows in St st, dec 1 st at end of every RS row—12 sts rem. Knit 1 WS row for turning ridge. Work 8 rows even in St st. Loosely BO all sts.

lower diagonal edge

With CC2, smaller needle, and RS facing, pick up and knit 39 (45, 51) sts evenly spaced along lower diagonal edge. Purl 1 WS row. Change to MC1 and work 11 rows even in St st. Knit 1 WS row for turning ridge. Work 12 more rows even in St st. Loosely BO all sts.

Fold all bindings to WS and, with sharp-point sewing needle and matching thread, sew in place. Butt collar binding edges to diagonal binding edges and with MC1 threaded on a tapestry needle, sew tog as invisibly as possible. With sharp-point sewing needle and matching thread, sew collar facing to WS.

Armhole Binding

Butt tog exposed edges of armhole steek and sew tog at shoulder. With CC2, smaller dpn, RS facing, and beg at center of right underarm, k12 held underarm sts, then pick up and knit 98 sts evenly spaced around armhole between steek and body sts, then k12 rem held underarm sts—122 sts total. Pm and join for working in rnds. Knit 1 rnd. Change to MC1 and knit 5 rnds, purl 1 rnd for turning ridge, then knit 6 rnds for facing. Loosely BO all sts. With sharp-point sewing needle and matching thread, sew armhole facing to WS. Overlap lower diagonal edge facing on top of upper diagonal edge facing. Butt edge against armhole facing and sew in place. Pick up and work sts on left armhole as for right armhole.

Hem Vents

Machine stitch and cut hem vents from lower edge of hem facing to end of Lotus chart patt. With CC2, smaller needle, RS facing, and beg at turning ridge on hem, pick up and knit 36 sts evenly spaced to top of vent. Purl 1 row. Change to MC1 and work 5 rows even in St st. Knit 1 WS row for turning ridge, then work 6 more rows in St st for facing. Loosely BO all sts. With sharp-point sewing needle and matching thread, sew vent facing to WS. Rep for opposite half of same vent. Rep for other hem vent.

Fold lower edge at turning ridge and sew facing to WS. Weave in loose ends. Block again if desired. Mark position for 3 closures evenly spaced along lower diagonal binding and 3 closures on right front opposite first closures. With sharp-point sewing needle and matching thread, sew in place. Sew snap to right center front below collar at pick-up row of binding.

STAR

"Velvet faces in the garden,
Blue and yellow at my door,
Johnny Jump-Ups sing of springtime,
Think of winter nevermore."

—Anonymous

johnny jump-up

FINISHED SIZE

About 11" (28 cm) circumference and 13½" (34.5 cm) long. To fit a child.

YARN

DK weight (#3 Light).

Shown here: Filatura di Crosa Zara (100% superwash merino; 137 yd [125 m]/50 g): #1740 deep violet (MC), 2 balls; #1493 crimson (CC1), #1745 deep olive (CC2), #1451 oatmeal (CC3), #1752 yellow (CC4), #1723 petunia (pink; CC5), and #1755 violet (CC6), 1 ball each.

NEEDLES

Ribbing: size U.S. 3 (3.25 mm): 16" (40 cm) circular (cir).
Leg warmer: size U.S. 5 (3.75 mm): 16" (40 cm) cir. Adjust needle size if necessary to obtain the correct gauge.

NOTIONS

Markers (m); tapestry needle; 1 yd (1 m) of 1¼" (3.2 cm) bias tape or ribbon; sharp-point sewing needle and matching thread.

GAUGE

26 stitches and 32 rounds = 4" (10 cm) in charted pattern on larger needle, worked in rounds.

The little ice skaters were clustered around their coach like petals on a flower. "One, two, three, JUMP!" she urged them. Again and again, tiny legs propelled skaters skyward, just like spring flowers leaping from the earth. Velvet faces that weren't there yesterday somehow smile up at me today. Knitting these leg warmers two at a time will prepare you nicely for knitting sleeves the same way.

Sometimes it can be easier to cut a steek from the wrong (non-public) side of the work where the machine stitching is more visible. Just turn the work inside out before you cut.

LEG WARMERS

Note: Both leg warmers are worked simultaneously as described on page 122.

Bottom Ribbing

With smaller needle, MC, and using the tubulan 1x1 rib method (see Glossary), CO 72 sts. Do not join. Work back and forth in k1, p1 rib until piece measures 2½" (6.5 cm) from CO, ending with a WS row. Set aside. Make another piece exactly the same. Change to larger needle.

Legs

Work Row 1 of Johnny Jump-Up chart across 72 sts of one piece, place marker (pm), use the backward-loop method (see Glossary) to CO 6 sts for steek (see page 124; these sts are not included in st counts unless otherwise indicated), pm, work Row 1 of Johnny Jump-Up chart across 72 sts of other piece, pm, use the backward-loop method to CO 6 sts for steek (these sts are not included in st counts unless otherwise indicated), pm, and join for working in rnds, being careful not to twist sts. Work Rows 2–39 of chart, then rep Rows 1–39 once more—piece measures about 12¼" (31 cm) from CO. Change to CC1 and knit 1 rnd. **Dividing row:** K72, BO 6 steek sts, k72, BO 6 steek sts—72 sts rem for each leg warmer.

Top Ribbing

With smaller needle and MC, work first set of 72 sts back and forth in k1, p1 rib for 1" (2.5 cm). Loosely BO all sts. Join MC to rem 72 leg sts and work back and forth in k1, p1 rib for 1" (2.5 cm). Loosely BO all sts.

FINISHING

With CC4 threaded on a tapestry needle, work 3 duplicate sts (see Glossary) for each flower center as indicated on chart. Block to measurements. Machine stitch and cut steeks as described on pages 125–127 to separate leg warmers. With MC threaded on a tapestry needle, sew seams. Weave in loose ends. With sharp-point sewing needle and matching thread, sew bias tape or ribbon over steek edges on WS of leg warmers.

Johnny Jump-Up

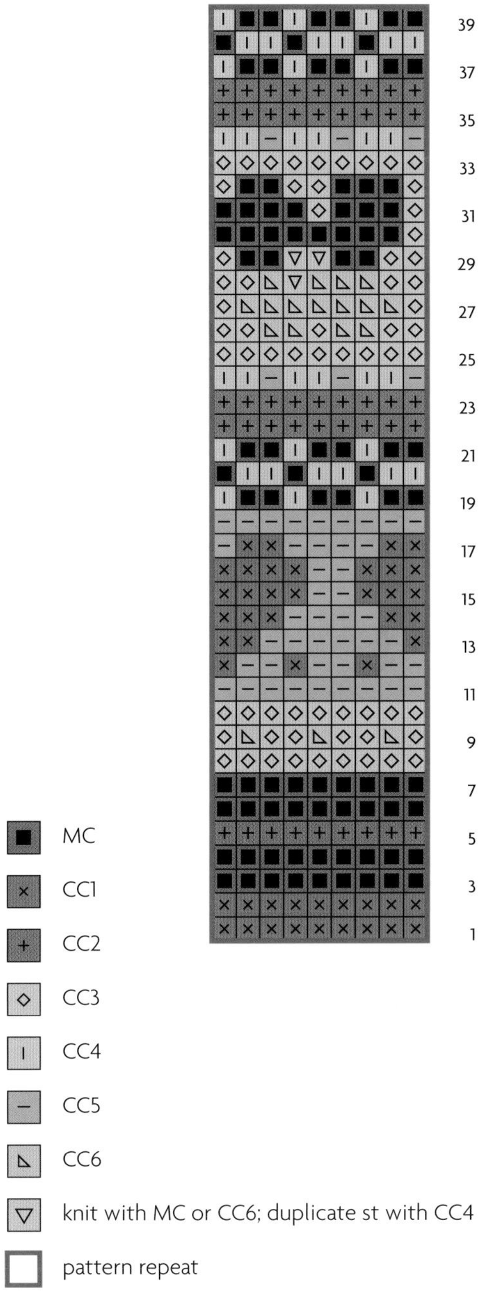

"My dame should dress in cheap attire
(Good, heavy silks are never dear);
I own perhaps I MIGHT desire
Some shawls of true Cashmere..."

—Oliver Wendell Holmes, *Contentment*

The pattern we commonly refer to as Paisley today is known by many names: Boteh, Palme, Welsh pears, and Persian pickles. Kashmir shawls, as they were originally called, were made by hand by skilled weavers over the course of many days. It was only after the invention of the Jacquard loom that the town of Paisley in Scotland claimed leadership in the mass production of the beautiful woolens. This cardigan is my homage to the tradition of the Paisley shawl. Its softly heathered yarn lends the colors a blended quality without sacrificing stitch definition. A combination of trims, closures, and French-knot accents creates additional surface dimension.

kashmir

FINISHED SIZE

About 34½ (37, 39½)" (87.5 [94, 100.5] cm) chest circumference. Sweater shown measures 39½" (100.5 cm).

YARN

Sportweight (#2 Fine).

Shown here: Reynolds Whiskey (100% wool; 195 yd [178 m]/50 g): #11 crimson (MC), 5 balls for all sizes; #16 burgundy (CC1), 1 (1, 2) ball(s); #103 light olive (CC2), #101 gold (CC3), and #53 teal (CC4), 1 ball each for all sizes.

NEEDLES

Body and sleeves: size U.S. 5 (3.75 mm): 16" (40 cm) and 24" (60 cm) circular (cir). *Hem facings:* size U.S. 3 (3.25 mm): 24" (60 cm) cir. Adjust needle size if necessary to obtain the correct gauge.

NOTIONS

Stitch holders or waste yarn; markers (m); tapestry needle; sharp-point sewing needle and matching thread; five 3½" (9 cm) frog closures; 1½ yd (1.4 m) each of three ribbon/braid trims: ¼" (6 mm), ½" (1.3 cm) and 1" (2.5 cm) wide (optional); 1½ yd (1.4 m) of 1" (2.5 cm) bias tape or ribbon to cover sleeve seams; thirty 6mm silver beads to embellish frogs.

GAUGE

26 stitches and 30 rounds = 4" (10 cm) in charted pattern on larger needle, worked in rounds.

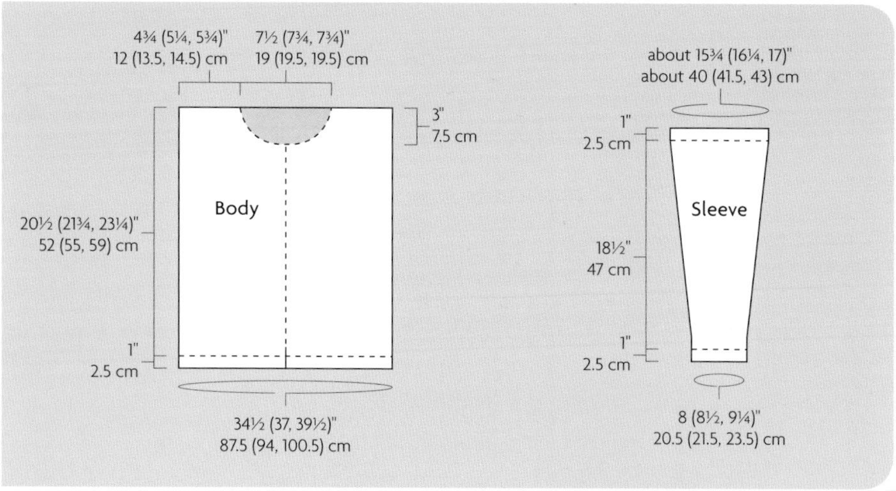

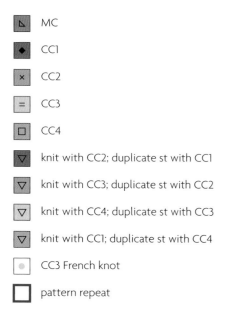

- MC
- CC1
- CC2
- CC3
- CC4
- knit with CC2; duplicate st with CC1
- knit with CC3; duplicate st with CC2
- knit with CC4; duplicate st with CC3
- knit with CC1; duplicate st with CC4
- CC3 French knot
- pattern repeat

Sew a coordinating metal or glass seed bead over too-obvious holes in metal clasps or buttons.

Mini Paisley

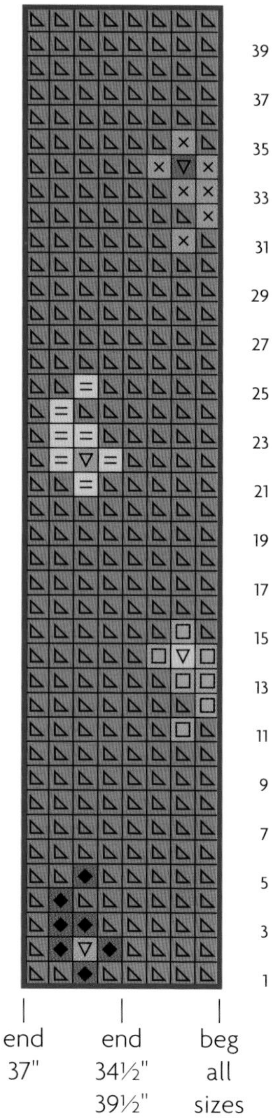

Large Paisley

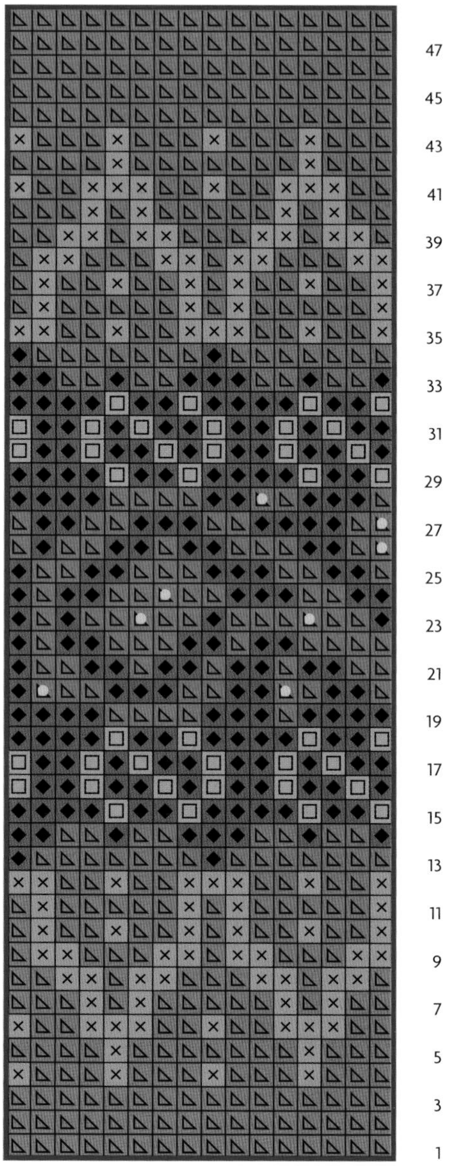

BODY

With MC and smaller cir needle, CO 224 (240, 256) sts. Work in St st back and forth in rows for 6 rows. Change to CC1 and knit 2 rows (purl ridge will form on RS for turning ridge). Change to MC and larger needle and work even in St st for 7 rows. **Joining rnd:** Place marker (pm), use the backward-loop method (see Glossary) to CO 6 steek sts (see page 124; these sts are not included in st counts unless otherwise indicated), pm, join for working in rnds. Work Rows 1–48 of Large Paisley chart. Work Rows 1–40 of Mini Paisley chart 2 times, then work Rows 1–18 (1–28, 1–38) once more—piece measures about 20½ (21¾, 23)" (52 [55, 58.5] cm) from turning ridge.

Place Stitches on Holders

With MC and beg at center of front steek, BO 3 steek sts, k20 (21, 21) and place these sts on a holder for right center front, k31 (34, 38) and place these sts on another holder for right front shoulder, BO 6 sts for top of right armhole opening, k31 (34, 38) and place these sts on another holder for right back shoulder, k48 (50, 50) and place these sts on another holder for back neck, k31 (34, 38) and place these sts on another holder for left back shoulder, BO 6 sts for top of left armhole opening, k31 (34, 38) and place these sts on another holder for left front shoulder, k20 (21, 21) and place these sts on another holder for left center front, BO rem 3 steek sts.

SLEEVES

Note: Both sleeves are worked simultaneously as described on page 122.

Cuffs

With MC and smaller needle, CO 52 (56, 60) sts. Work in St st back and forth in rows for 7 rows. Knit 1 WS row for turning ridge. Change to CC1 and larger needle and work 7 rows in St st. Cut off yarn. Place sts on holder. Make a second cuff the same. **Joining rnd:** With larger, shorter cir needle and RS facing, join MC and knit across first cuff, pm, use the backward-loop method to CO 6 steek sts, pm, with the same yarn, knit across second cuff, pm, CO 6 steek sts, pm, and join for working in rnds, being careful not to twist sts—52 (56, 60) sts for each sleeve, 6 steek sts between sleeves.

Work 2 rnds even in St st. Inc 1 st each side of marker every 5th rnd to end of sleeve, working new sts into patt. *At the same time* work Rows 1–40 of Mini Paisley chart 3 times, then work Rows 1–8 once more—piece measures 18¼" (46.5 cm) from turning ridge. Work additional rows of Mini Paisley chart to lengthen sleeve, if desired. **Next rnd:** Work across first sleeve sts and place these sts on a holder, BO 6 steek sts, work across second sleeve sts and place these sts on another holder, BO 6 steek sts.

FINISHING

With yarn threaded on a tapestry needle, work French knots and duplicate sts (see Glossary for embroidery sts) on body and sleeves as indicated on charts. With sharp-point sewing needle and matching thread, sew hems in place on WS. Block pieces to measurements.

Cut Steeks, Armholes, and Neckline

Machine stitch and cut center front steek and armhole openings as described on pages 125–127. Machine stitch and cut sleeve steeks to separate sleeves.

Machine stitch and cut front neckline curve to a depth of 3" (7.5 cm) as described on page 129.

Place 31 (34, 38) right front shoulder sts on one needle and corresponding 31 (34, 38) right back shoulder sts on another needle. With RS tog, use the three-needle method as described on page 130 to BO the shoulder sts tog. Rep for other shoulder.

Sleeve Facings

With MC threaded on a tapestry needle, sew underarm sleeve seams. Return held sleeve sts to larger, shorter cir needle. With MC, purl 6 rnds, inc 1 st at beg and end of each rnd. Loosely BO all sts. Cover seam on inside of sleeve with ribbon or bias tape as described on page 132.

Front Facing

With CC1, larger needle, and RS facing, pick up and knit 100 (107, 116) sts evenly spaced along right front edge between steek and body sts. Work 5 rows even in St st. Change to MC and smaller needle and knit 2 rows to form turning ridge. Change to CC1 and work 6 more rows even in St st. Loosely BO all sts. Turn facing to WS and, with sharp-point sewing needle and matching thread, sew to WS. Rep for left front edge.

Neck Facing

With MC, larger needle, and RS facing, pick up and knit 32 (33, 33) sts along right front neck edge, k48 (50, 50) held back neck sts, pick up and knit 32 (33, 33) sts along left front neck edge—112 (116, 116) sts total. Work 5 rows even in St st. Change to CC1 and smaller needle. Knit 2 rows to form turning ridge on RS. Change to MC and work 6 more rows even in St st. Loosely BO all sts. Turn facing to WS and sew in place with sharp-point sewing needle and matching thread.

Insert sleeves into armholes and sew in place, as described on page 132. Turn sleeve facings to WS and sew in place.

Apply optional ribbon/braid trim along side of front bands, placing 1" (2.5 cm) wide ribbon next to band, ¼" (6 mm) wide ribbon next to 1" (2.5 cm) ribbon, and ½" (1.3 cm) wide ribbon next to ¼" (6 mm) ribbon. Sew 3 silver beads to each half of each frog. Sew frogs to front, placing the highest on the pick-up rnd for the neck facing, the lowest 3" (7.5 cm) from the lower edge, and the others evenly spaced in between.

Cuffs and hems can easily be worked in the round, but I like to work them back and forth in rows because:

- *The small diameters of cuffs make them easier to work flat than in rounds.*
- *There's less chance of twisting the stitches when joining for working in rounds if there is already an inch or more of knitting on the needles.*

"The pedigree of honey
Does not concern the bee;
A clover, any time, to him
Is aristocracy."

—Emily Dickinson

I do love a good baby sweater. If you are lucky enough to have a small person in your life for whom you can knit, good on you. If you don't, I still encourage you to make a little sweater at least once. Here is why: If you are new to stranded colorwork, the level of commitment and expense are much lower than with a full-size work. If you are more experienced, the speed with which you complete your project will be extremely gratifying. In both cases, the finished object is so cute you will have lots of fun finding ways to display it. Who knows? You may even find a wee one to wear it for you one day. Send me pictures when you do!

the bees' knees

Finished Size

22½ (30)" (57 [76] cm) chest circumference.
Sweater shown measures 22½" (57 cm).

Yarn

Fingering weight (#1 Super Fine).
Shown here: Dale of Norway Baby Ull (100% superwash merino; 180 yd [165 m]/50 g): #2106 yellow (MC) and #3871 brown (CC1), 3 (4) balls each; #0020 cream (CC2) and #9436 green (CC3), 1 ball each for both sizes.

Needles

Body and sleeves: size U.S. 2 (2.75 mm): 24" (60 cm) circular (cir) and set of 4 or 5 double-pointed (dpn).
Facing: size U.S. 1 (2.25 mm): 24" (60 cm) cir and set of 4 or 5 dpn. Adjust needle size if necessary to obtain the correct gauge.

Notions

Stitch holders or waste yarn; markers (m); tapestry needle; sharp-point sewing needle and matching thread; five (seven) 1½" (3.8 cm) small pewter hooks; 1 yd (1 m) of 1" (2.5 cm) bias tape or ribbon to cover sleeve seams.

Gauge

32 stitches and 36 rounds = 4" (10 cm) in charted pattern on larger needle, worked in rounds.

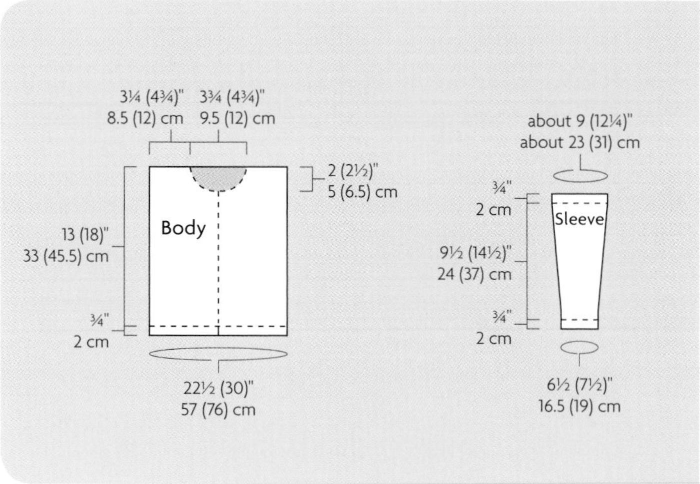

BODY

With CC3 and smaller cir needle, CO 180 (240) sts. Do not join. Work back and forth in St st for 6 rows for facing. **Picot row:** (RS) *K2tog, yo; rep from * to last 2 sts, k2tog—1 st dec'd. Change to larger cir needle. Work 6 rows in St st, inc 1 st at beg of first row—1 st inc'd. **Joining rnd:** Place marker (pm), use the backward-loop method (see Glossary) to CO 6 sts for center front steek (see page 124; these sts are not included in st counts unless otherwise indicated), pm, and join for working in rnds, being careful not to twist sts. Work Rows 1–11 of Pollen chart. Work Rows 1–25 of Big Bee chart. Rep Rows 1–10 of Honeycomb chart until piece measures about 10 (15)" (25.5 [38] cm) from picot row, ending with Row 4 or 9 of chart. Work Row 11 of Honeycomb chart. Work Rows 1–24 of Little Bee chart, ending last rnd at center of steek sts.

Place Stitches on Holders

With CC2, BO 3 steek sts, k15 (19) and place these sts on holder for right center front, k27 (38) and place these sts on a second holder for right front shoulder, BO 6 sts for top of right armhole, k27 (38) and place these sts on a third holder for right back shoulder, k30 (38) and place these sts on a fourth holder for back neck, k27 (38) and place these sts on a fifth holder for left back shoulder, BO 6 sts for top of left armhole, k27 (38) and place these sts on a sixth holder for left front shoulder, k15 (19) and place these sts on a seventh holder for left center front, BO rem 3 steek sts.

Big Bee

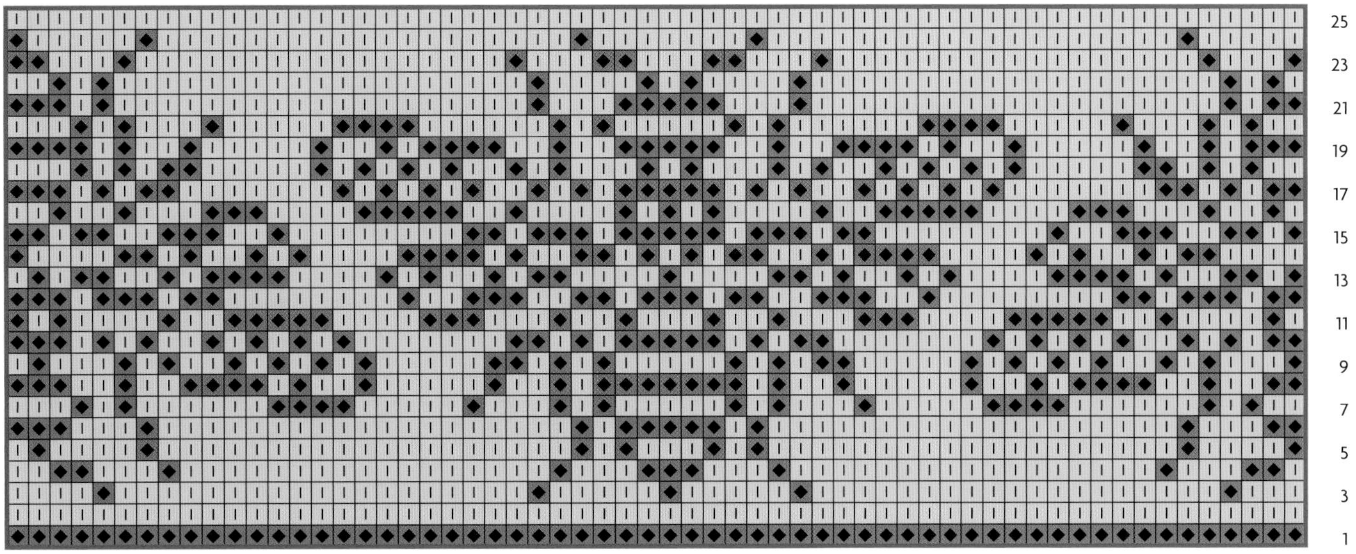

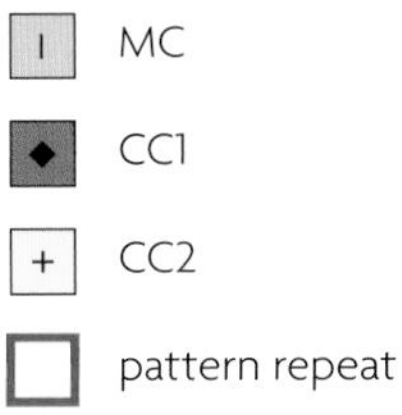

Pollen

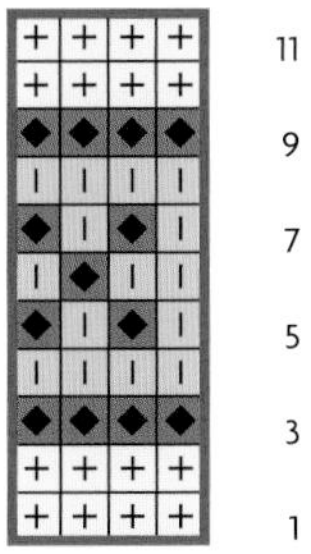

Little Bee

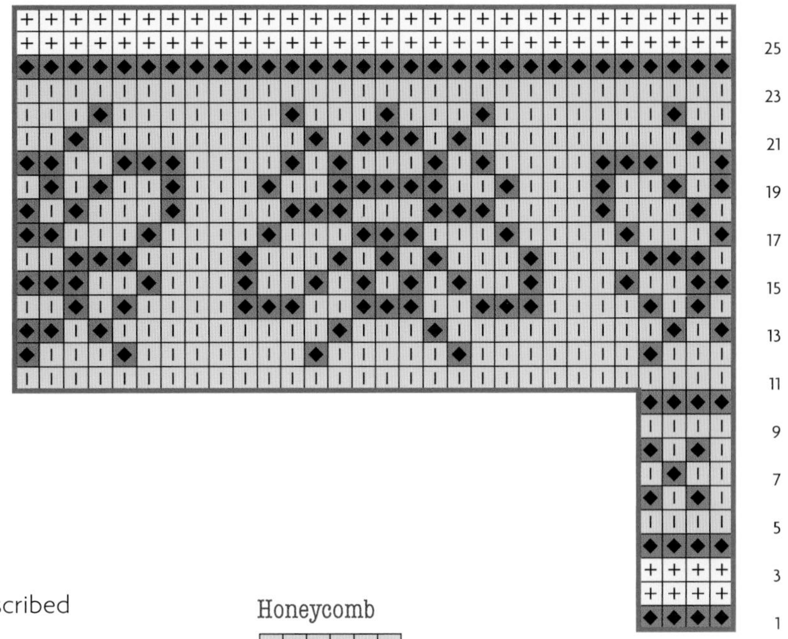

SLEEVES

Note: Both sleeves are worked simultaneously as described on page 122.

Cuffs

With CC3 and smaller needle, CO 52 (60) sts. Do not join. Work back and forth in St st for 6 rows. **Picot row:** (RS) *K2tog, yo; rep from * to last 2 sts, k2tog—1 st dec'd. Change to larger needle. Work 6 rows in St st, inc 1 st at beg of first row—1 st inc'd. Cut yarn. Place sts on holder. Make a second cuff to match.

Honeycomb

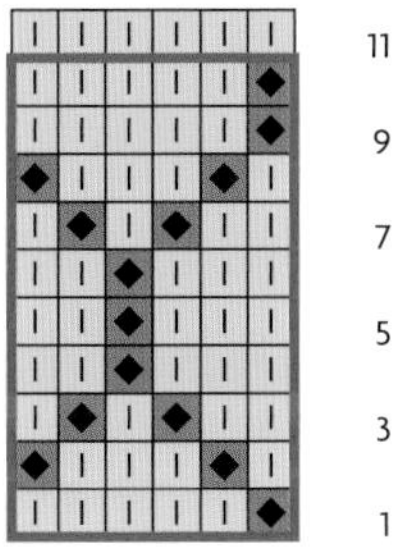

Join Sleeves

With CC3, larger dpn, and RS facing, knit across first cuff, pm, use the backward-loop method to CO 6 steek sts, pm, knit across second cuff, pm, use the backward-loop method to CO 6 steek sts, pm, and join for working in rnds, being careful not to twist sts—52 (60) sts for each sleeve, 6 steek sts between sleeves. Rep Rows 1–9 of Pollen chart, inc 1 st at beg and end of every 5th rnd on each sleeve (4 incs per inc rnd) until piece measures 6½ (11½)" (16.5 [29] cm) from picot row, working new sts into patt. Cont to inc every 5th rnd, work Rows 2–26 of Little Bee chart. **Next rnd:** Work across first sleeve sts and place these sts on a holder or waste yarn, BO 6 steek sts, work across second sleeve sts and place these sts on another holder, BO rem 6 steek sts.

FINISHING

Weave in loose ends. Block pieces to measurements.

Cut Steeks, Armhole Openings, and Neckline

Machine stitch and cut center front steek and armhole openings as described on pages 125–127. Machine stitch and cut sleeve steeks to separate sleeves. Machine stitch and cut front neckline curve to a depth of 2 (2½)" (5 [6.5] cm) as described on page 129. Turn each facing to WS along picot row and, with sharp-point sewing needle and matching thread, sew in place. Place 27 (38) held right front shoulder sts on one needle and the corresponding 27 (38) held right back shoulder sts on another needle. Hold needles parallel with RS tog and use the three-needle method as described on page 130 to BO the shoulder sts tog. Rep for left shoulder.

Front Facing

With CC2, smaller needle, and RS facing, pick up and knit 86 (126) sts evenly spaced along right front edge between steek and body sts. Working back and forth in St st, purl 1 (WS) row. Change to CC3 and work 5 rows. **Picot row:** (WS) *K2tog, yo; rep from * to last 2 sts, k2tog—1 st dec'd. Work 6 rows in St st, inc 1 st at beg of first row—1 st inc'd. Loosely BO all sts. Turn facing to WS and, with sharp-point sewing needle and matching thread, sew in place. Rep for left front facing.

Neck Facing

With CC2, smaller needle, and RS facing, pick up and knit 21 (25) sts along right front neck edge, k30 (38) held back neck sts, then pick up and knit 21 (25) sts along left front neck edge—72 (88) sts total. Working back and forth in St st, purl 1 (WS) row. Change to CC3 and work 5 rows. **Picot row:** (WS) *K2tog, yo; rep from * to

Consider the following when deciding to knit sleeves separately or together.

- *Will the extra bulk created by a seam in the sleeve create a problem? If so, work the sleeves separately.*
- *Will the cuff edge treatment be adversely affected by seaming? If so, work the sleeves separately.*
- *Does a noticeable jog form at the boundary between rounds? This is especially a problem with stripes. If so, consider working the sleeves together.*

last 2 sts, k2tog—1 st dec'd. Work 6 rows in St st, inc 1 st at beg of first row—1 st inc'd. Loosely BO all sts. Turn facing to WS and sew in place.

Sleeve Facing

With MC threaded on a tapestry needle, sew sleeve seams. Place held sts for one sleeve on smaller dpn. Pm and join for working in rnds. With MC, purl 6 rnds, inc 1 st each side of marker every rnd. BO all sts. Cover seam on inside of sleeve with ribbon or bias tape as described on page 132. Rep for other sleeve.

Insert sleeves into armholes and sew in place as described on page 132. Turn facings to WS to cover cut edges of openings and sew in place. Apply pewter hooks evenly spaced along front opening.

"Until either black stripes or white stripes can win you / The battle for which stripes are which will continue."

— Anonymous

fleur de zebra

FINISHED SIZE

41¼ (46¼, 51½)" (105 [117.5, 131] cm) chest circumference. Sweater shown measures 41¼" (105 cm).

YARN

Sportweight (#2 Fine).

Shown here: Filatura Di Crosa Zarina (100% superwash merino; 180 yd [165 m]/50 g): #1396 off-white (MC) and #1404 black (CC1), 6 (7, 8) balls each; #1723 bubblegum pink (CC2), 1 (2, 2) balls.

NEEDLES

Body and sleeves: size U.S. 4 (3.5 mm): 24" (60 cm) cir and set of 4 or 5 double-pointed (dpn). *Edging:* size U.S. 3 (3.25 mm): 24" (60 cm) cir and set of 4 or 5 dpn. Adjust needle size if necessary to obtain the correct gauge.

NOTIONS

Stitch holders or waste yarn; markers (m); tapestry needle; sharp-point sewing needle and matching thread; six ⅞" (2.2 cm) buttons; ½ yd (.5 m) of ⅞" (2.2 cm) wide bias tape.

GAUGE

28 stitches and 32 rounds = 4" (10 cm) in charted pattern on larger needle, worked in rounds.

A lot of opinions have been offered on the subject of why zebra are striped. Rather than venture my own guess, I will just celebrate their beauty. The graphic quality of black and white appeals to me as much as the zebra's exotic cache. A shot of pink provides the surprise finishing touch.

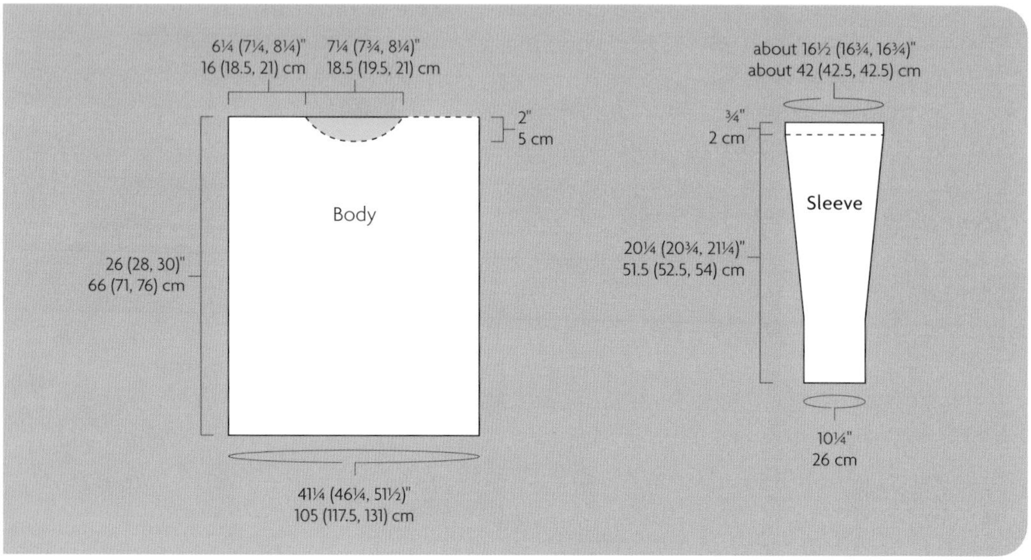

6¼ (7¼, 8¼)"
16 (18.5, 21) cm
7¼ (7¾, 8¼)"
18.5 (19.5, 21) cm
2"
5 cm
Body
26 (28, 30)"
66 (71, 76) cm
41¼ (46¼, 51½)"
105 (117.5, 131) cm
about 16½ (16¾, 16¾)"
about 42 (42.5, 42.5) cm
¾"
2 cm
Sleeve
20¼ (20¾, 21¼)"
51.5 (52.5, 54) cm
10¼"
26 cm

STITCH GUIDE

Picot Cast-On

Using the cable method (see Glossary), *CO 5 sts, BO 2 sts; rep from * until there are the desired number of sts.

Picot Bind-Off

Using the cable method, *CO 2 sts, BO 5 sts; rep from * to last 3, 2 or 1 st(s), CO 2 sts, BO rem sts.

Zebra

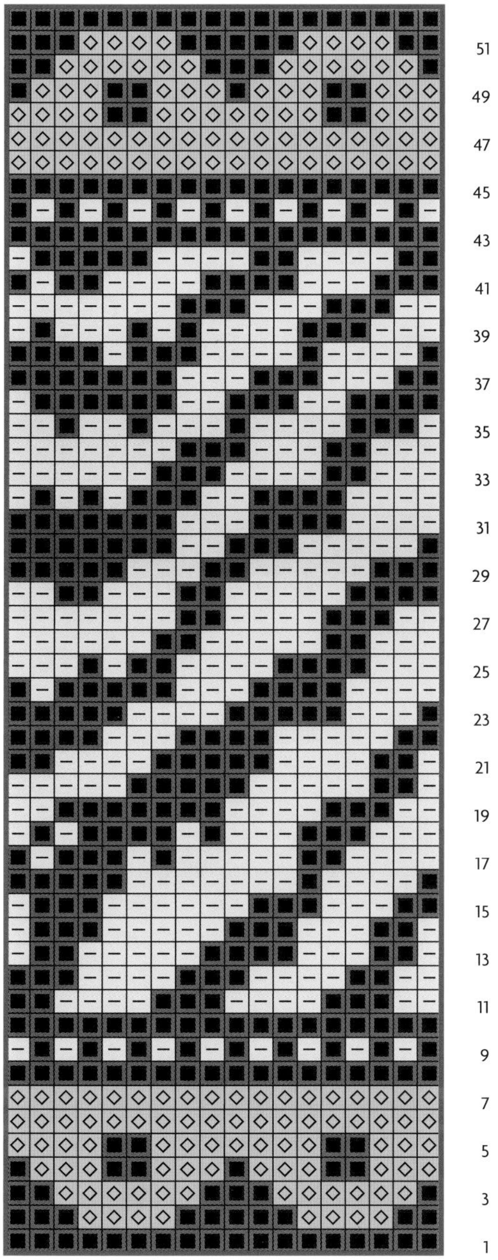

BODY

With CC2, smaller cir needle, and using the picot method (see Stitch Guide at left), CO 288 (324, 360) sts. Place marker (pm) and join for working in rnds, being careful not to twist sts. Change to larger cir needle and CC1. Knit 1 rnd. Work in k2, p2 rib for 1" (2.5 cm). Work Rows 1–52 of Zebra chart. Change to Fleur de Lis chart and rep Rows 1–24 until piece measures 25½ (27½, 29½)" (65 [70, 75] cm) from CO. Work Rows 1–4 of Stripes chart (do not work Rows 5 and 6 of chart).

Place Stitches on Holders

With CC2, BO 3 sts for half of top of left armhole, k44 (51, 58) and place these sts on a holder for left front shoulder, k50 (54, 58) and place these sts on another holder for center front, k44 (51, 58) and place these sts on another holder for right front shoulder, BO 6 sts for top of right armhole, k44 (51, 58) and place these sts on another holder for right back shoulder, k50 (54, 58) and place these sts on another holder for back neck, k44 (51, 58) and place these sts on another holder for left back shoulder, BO 3 sts for other half of top of left armhole.

Use easy-release painters' tape to mark your place on charts and to secure yarn tails when you machine stitch and cut steeks. (It also comes in handy for quieting loved ones who insist you already have enough yarn.)

- (–) MC
- (■) CC1
- (◇) CC2
- (□) pattern repeat

Stripes

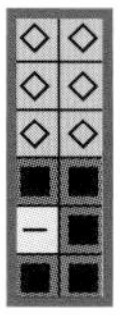

- MC
- CC1
- CC2
- pattern repeat

Fluer de Lis

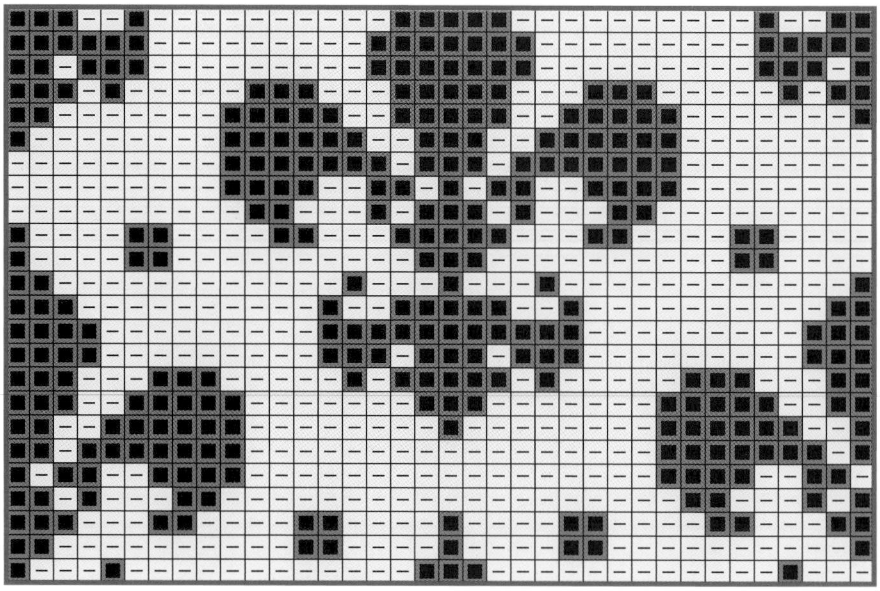

SLEEVES (make 2)

With CC2, smaller dpn, and using the picot method, CO 72 sts. Pm and join for working in rnds, being careful not to twist sts. Change to larger dpn and CC1 and knit 1 rnd. Work in k2, p2 rib for 1" (2.5 cm). Work Rows 1–26, then Rows 43–52 (i.e., do not work Rows 27–42) of Zebra chart. Rep Rows 1–24 of Fleur de Lis chart and *at the same time* inc 1 st each side of marker every 5th rnd, working new sts into patt, until piece measures 19½ (20, 20½)" (49.5 [51, 52] cm) from CO. Work Rows 1–6 of Stripes chart. With MC, purl 6 rnds for facing, inc 1 st each side of marker every rnd. Loosely BO all sts.

FINISHING

Weave in loose ends. Block pieces to measurements.

Cut Armholes and Neckline

Mark, machine stitch, and cut armhole openings as described on pages 125–127. Mark, machine stitch, and cut front neckline curve to a depth of 2" (5 cm) as described on page 129. Place 44 (51, 58) held right front shoulder sts on one needle and corresponding 44 (51, 58) held right back shoulder sts on another needle. With RS tog, use the three-needle method as described on page 130 to BO the shoulder sts tog.

Turtleneck

With CC1, smaller needle, and RS facing, pick up and knit 54 (58, 62) sts evenly spaced around front neck, then k50 (54, 58) held back neck sts—104 (112, 120) sts total. Working back and forth in rows, work in k2, p2 rib until turtleneck measures 3" (7.5 cm) from pick-up row. Change to larger needle and cont in k2, p2 rib until turtleneck measures 6" (15 cm) from pick-up row, ending with a RS row. (**Note:** RS of turtleneck will be on the inside of garment, due to fold-over.) Change to CC2 and purl 1 row. Change to smaller needle. Using the picot method (see Stitch Guide on page 83), BO all sts. Fold over turtleneck, matching side edges.

Button Placket

back edge facing

With CC1, smaller needle, RS facing, and beg at folded edge, pick up and knit 24 sts through both layers of turtleneck at left back edge, then k44 (51, 58) held left back shoulder sts—68 (75, 82) sts total. Work 5 rows even in St st. Purl 1 RS row for turning ridge. Work 6 more rows in St st. Loosely BO all sts. Fold placket along turning ridge and, with sharp-point sewing needle and matching thread, sew facing to WS.

front edge facing

With CC2, smaller needle, and RS facing, p44 (51, 58) held front shoulder sts, change to CC1 and pick up and purl 24 sts through both layers of folded turtleneck—68 (75, 82) sts total. Maintaining colors as established, work 6 rows in St st. Loosely BO all sts. Fold facing to WS and sew in place.

Cover front neckline cut edge with bias tape as described on page 132. Butt edges of left armhole tog and, with sharp-point sewing needle and matching thread, sew tog at shoulder.

With sharp-point sewing needle and matching thread, sew 6 buttons evenly spaced onto back placket. Make 6 button loops opposite buttons as foll: Join CC1 to front placket edge. Make a loop of yarn large enough to accommodate button; take a st in front placket edge to secure. Work buttonhole st (see Glossary) over loop to strengthen. Rep for rem buttons.

Insert sleeves into armholes and sew in place as described on page 132. Fold sleeve facing to WS to cover cut edges of openings and, with sharp-point sewing needle and matching thread, sew in place.

"In every painting a whole is mysteriously enclosed, a whole life of tortures, doubts, of hours of enthusiasm and inspiration."

—Wassily Kandinsky

A friend of mine once bought a dog-eared poster at a sidewalk sale. It was an art print that only needed framing to legitimize it. I had never heard of the artist, but I was drawn to the picture's kinetic energy and stunning colors. To me, it was modern in every way. Little did I know then that it had been painted some eighty years before. There is nothing new under the sun; all music is made from the same few notes. The great artists seem always to be asking themselves: What will I make today that has never been seen before?

wassily vest

FINISHED SIZE

44¼ (46¾, 49)" (112.5 [118.5, 124.5] cm) chest circumference. Vest shown measures 46¾" (118.5 cm).

YARN

DK weight (#3 Light).

Shown here: Classic Elite Wool Bam Boo (50% wool, 50% bamboo; 118 yd [108 m]/50 g): #1627 mulled wine (MC), 8 (8, 9) balls; #1635 key lime (CC1), #1689 watermelon (CC2), #1658 tomato (CC3), #1691 bay blue (CC4), #1695 plum (CC5), #1605 sachet (lavender; CC6), and #1615 ivy (CC7), 1 ball each for all sizes.

NEEDLES

Body and rolled hems: size U.S. 5 (3.75 mm): 24" and 16" (60 and 40 cm) circular (cir). *Ribbing:* size U.S. 4 (3.5 mm): 24" (60 cm) and two 16" (40 cm) cir. Adjust needle size if necessary to obtain the correct gauge.

NOTIONS

Stitch holders or waste yarn; markers (m); tapestry needle; sharp-point sewing needle and matching thread; three ⅞" (2.2 cm) buttons; 1 sew-on snap.

GAUGE

24 stitches and 28 rounds = 4" (10 cm) in charted pattern on larger needle, worked in rounds.

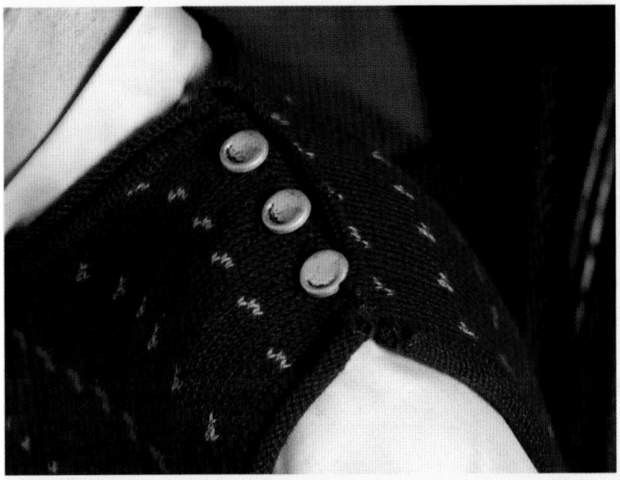

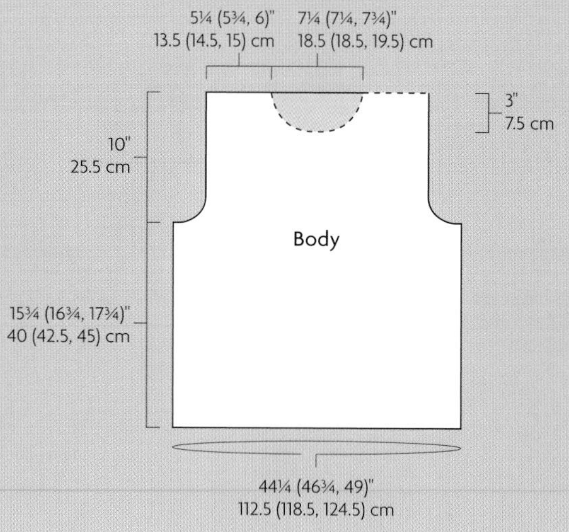

BODY

With larger needle and MC, CO 266 (280, 294) sts. Place marker (pm) and join for working in rnds, being careful not to twist sts. Rnd begs at left side "seam." Knit 1 rnd and pm after 133 (140, 147) sts to denote other side "seam." Knit 5 more rnds. Change to smaller needle and work 2 rnds in k1, p1 rib. Change to larger needle and, beg and ending as indicated for your size, work Rows 1 and 2 of Boxes chart. Work Rows 1–36 of Wassily Border chart, then work Rows 1–37 of Body Chart 1, then work Rows 1–52 of Body Chart 2, then rep Rows 1–67 of Body Chart 3 (see page 90) as needed to top of shoulder and *at the same time* beg armhole shaping when piece measures 15 (16, 17)" (38 [40.5, 43] cm) from top of k1, p1 rib.

Shape Armholes

Place last 7 sts onto waste yarn or holder, k7 and place these sts onto the same holder (14 sts on holder), work to m, place last 7 sts onto waste yarn or holder, k7 and place these sts onto same holder, work to end of rnd—238 (252, 266) sts rem; 119 (126, 133) sts each for front and back. **Next rnd:** Pm, use the backward-loop method (see Glossary) to CO 6 sts for armhole steek (see page 124; steek sts are not included in st counts unless otherwise indicated), pm, work to second armhole in patt, pm, use the backward-loop method to CO 6 steek sts, pm, work to end of rnd. **Dec rnd:** Keeping in patt, work the 6 steek sts, k3, ssk, knit to 5 sts before armhole, k2tog, k3, work 6 steek sts, k3, ssk, knit to 5 sts before next armhole, k2tog, k3—4 sts dec'd. Work 1 rnd even in patt. Rep the last 2 rnds 6 more times—210 (224, 238) sts rem; 105 (112, 119) sts each for front and back. Cont even in patt until armholes measure 10" (25.5 cm), ending at center of left armhole steek.

Wassily Border

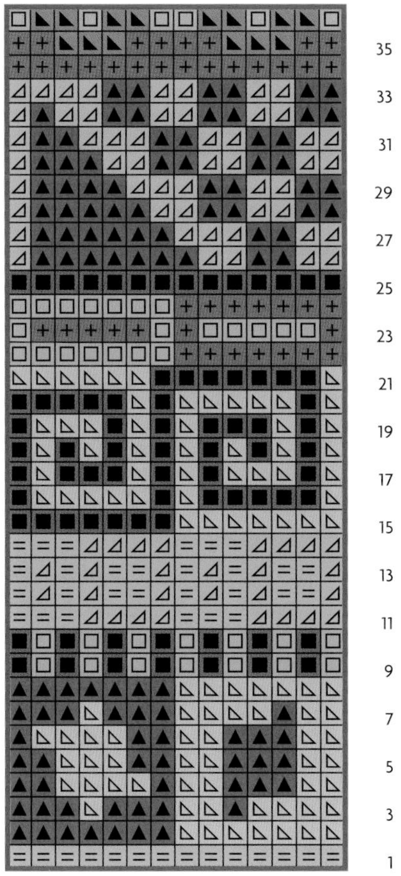

Body Chart 1

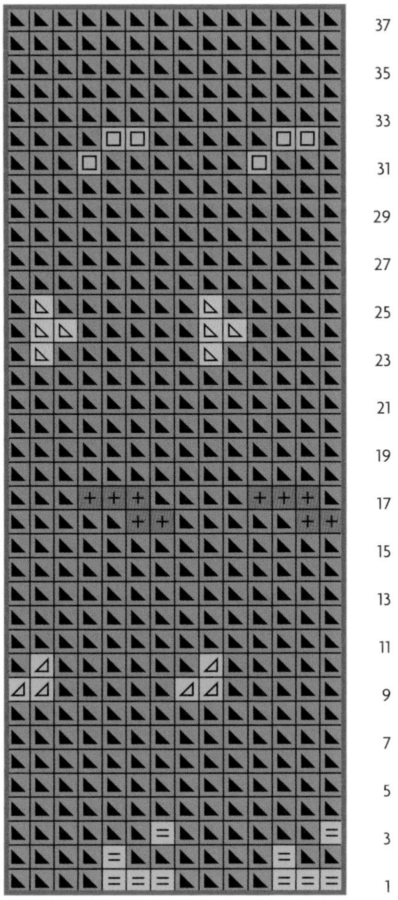

Body Chart 2

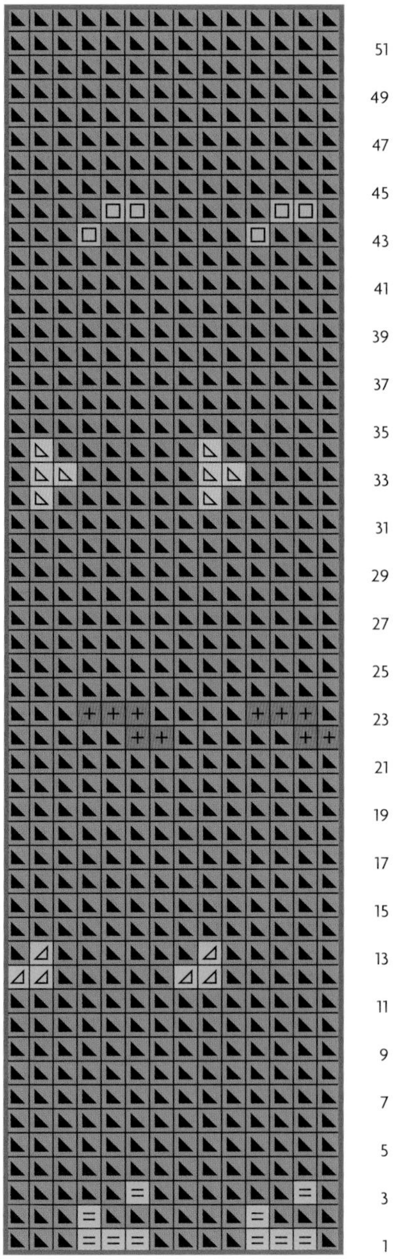

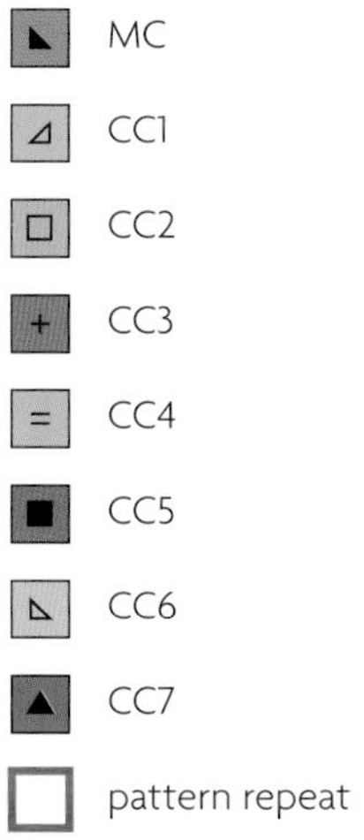

Boxes

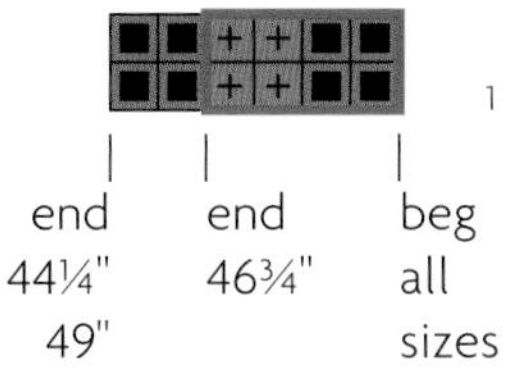

Body Chart 3

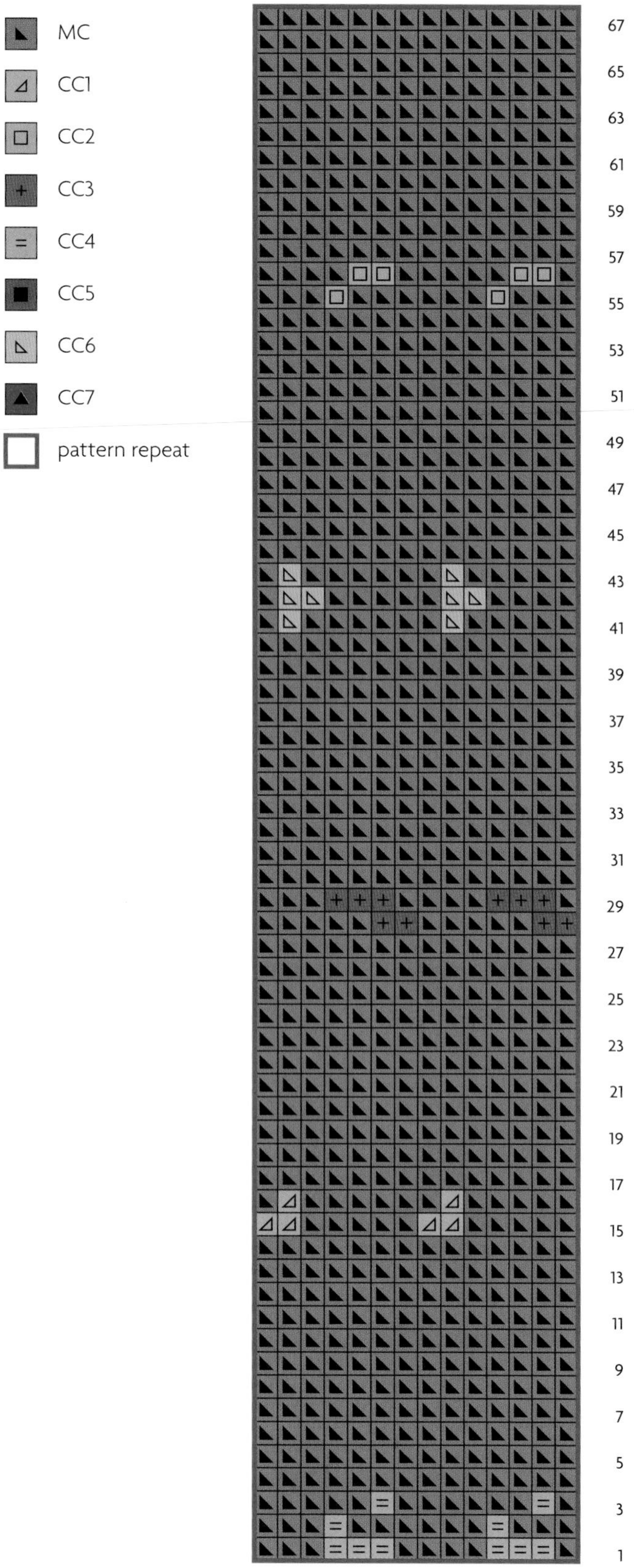

Place Stitches on Holders

With MC, BO 3 left armhole steek sts, k31 (34, 36) and place these sts on a holder for left front shoulder, k43 (44, 47) and place these sts on a second holder for front neck, k31 (34, 36) and place these sts on a third holder for right front shoulder, BO 6 sts for right armhole steek, k31 (34, 36) and place these sts on a fourth holder for right back shoulder, k43 (44, 47) and place these sts on a fifth holder for back neck, k31 (34, 36) and place these sts on a sixth holder for left back shoulder, BO 3 rem left armhole steek sts.

FINISHING

Weave in loose ends. Block to measurements.

Cut Steeks and Neckline

Mark, machine stitch, and cut armhole steeks as described on pages 125–127. Mark, machine stitch, and cut front neckline curve to a depth of 3" (7.5 cm) as described on page 129. Place 31 (34, 36) held right front shoulder sts on one needle and the corresponding 31 (34, 36) held right back shoulder sts on another needle. Hold the needles parallel with RS facing tog and use the three-needle method as described on page 130 to join the shoulder sts tog.

Right Armhole

With MC, smaller needle, and RS facing, k14 held sts at bottom of armhole, then pick up and knit 102 sts evenly spaced around armhole between steek and body sts—116 sts total. Pm and join for working in rnds. Knit 5 rnds. With another smaller needle and WS facing, pick up and knit 1 st under each running thread created by first picked-up sts, then 1 st under each running thread created by knitting held sts—116 sts total. Pm and join for working in rnds. Knit 4 rnds. With first needle and RS facing, *knit 1 st from first needle tog with 1 st from second needle; rep from * until all sts are joined—116 sts. Change to larger needle and knit 6 rnds. Loosely BO all sts.

Left Shoulder Button Placket

With MC, smaller needle, and beg with RS facing, work 31 (34, 36) held left back shoulder sts in St st for 5 rows. Knit 1 (WS) row for turning ridge. Work 4 more rows in St st for facing. BO all sts. Turn facing to WS and with sharp-point sewing needle and matching thread, sew in place.

Buttonhole Band

With MC, smaller needle, and WS facing, p31 (34, 36) held left front shoulder sts. With RS facing, k6 (6, 7), BO 3 sts, k5 (6, 7), BO 3 sts, k5 (6, 7), BO 3 sts, k6 (7, 6). **Next row:** K6 (7, 6), use the backward-loop method to CO 3 sts to complete buttonhole, k5 (6, 7), CO 3 sts, k5 (6, 7), CO 3 sts, k6 (6, 7). Work 2 rows in St st. Work 2 rows k1, p1 rib. Change to larger needle and work 6 rows in St st. BO all sts.

Left Armhole

With smaller needle, MC, and RS facing, pick up and knit 53 sts evenly spaced along back armhole edge between steek and body sts, k14 held sts at base of armhole, then pick up and knit 53 sts evenly spaced along front armhole edge between steek and body sts—120 sts total. Work 5 rows even in St st. With another smaller needle and WS facing, pick up and knit 1 st under each running thread created by first picked-up sts, 1 st under each running thread created by knitting held sts, then 1 st under each running thread created by first picked-up sts—120 sts total. Beg with a WS row, work 4 rows in St st. With first needle and RS facing, *knit 1 st from first needle tog with 1 st from second needle; rep from * until all sts are joined—120 sts. Change to larger needle and work 6 rows in St st. BO all sts.

Neckline

With MC, smaller needle, RS facing, and beg at left front shoulder edge, pick up and knit 64 (66, 70) sts evenly spaced around front neck edge, k43 (44, 47) held back neck sts—107 (110, 117) sts total. Do not join. Work 5 rows in St st. With another smaller needle and WS facing, pick up and knit 1 st under each running thread created by knitting held sts, then 1 st under each running thread created by first picked-up sts—107 (110, 117) sts total. Beg with a WS row, work 4 rows in St st. With first needle and RS facing, *knit 1 st from first needle tog with 1 st from second needle; rep from * until all sts are joined—107 (110, 117) sts. Change to larger needle and work 6 rows in St st. BO all sts.

Sew buttons to placket opposite buttonholes. Sew snap in place at neck edge near left shoulder.

"I met a lady in the meads,
Full beautiful—a faery's child,
Her hair was long, her foot was light,
And her eyes were wild."
—John Keats, *La Belle Dame Sans Merci*

wedding belle

FINISHED SIZE
About 35¾ (39, 42¼)" (91 [99, 107.5] cm) bust circumference. Sweater shown measures 35¾" (91 cm).

YARN
Fingering weight (#1 Super Fine).
Shown here: Dale of Norway Baby Ull (100% wool; 180 yd [165 m]/50 g): #2425 off-white (MC), 9 (10, 10) balls; #2621 pale tan (CC1), 2 balls for all sizes; #4711 light pink (CC2) and #4504 medium pink (CC3), 1 ball each for all sizes.

NEEDLES
Body and sleeves: size U.S. 2 (2.75 mm): 24" (60 cm) circular (cir) and set of 4 or 5 double-pointed (dpn). *Binding:* size U.S. 1 (2.25 mm): 24" (60 cm) cir and set of 4 or 5 dpn. *Lace cuffs:* size U.S. 3 (3.25 mm): set of 4 or 5 dpn. Adjust needle size if necessary to obtain the correct gauge.

NOTIONS
Stitch holders or waste yarn; markers (m); tapestry needle; sharp-point sewing needle and matching thread; 1½ yd (1.4 m) each of 3 ribbon or braid trims: ⅜" (1 cm), ½" (1.3 cm), and 1¾" (4.5 cm) wide (optional); five 2½" (6.5 cm) metal clasps.

GAUGE
32 stitches and 39 rounds = 4" (10 cm) in charted pattern on middle-size needle, worked in rounds.

A haute-couture fashion-show tradition is for the last outfit down the runway to be a wedding garment. Some of these creations have been notable, if not always conventional or wearable. It's a grand custom, though, and as a nod to that ritual, I have saved this cardigan for last. The fashion in wedding gowns in my part of the country has favored sleeveless and strapless frocks for several seasons now. For this merry confection, I wanted to create something special and warm for the bridal ensemble, having attended more than one wedding reception where the bride had to don the groom's tuxedo jacket to keep frostbite at bay.

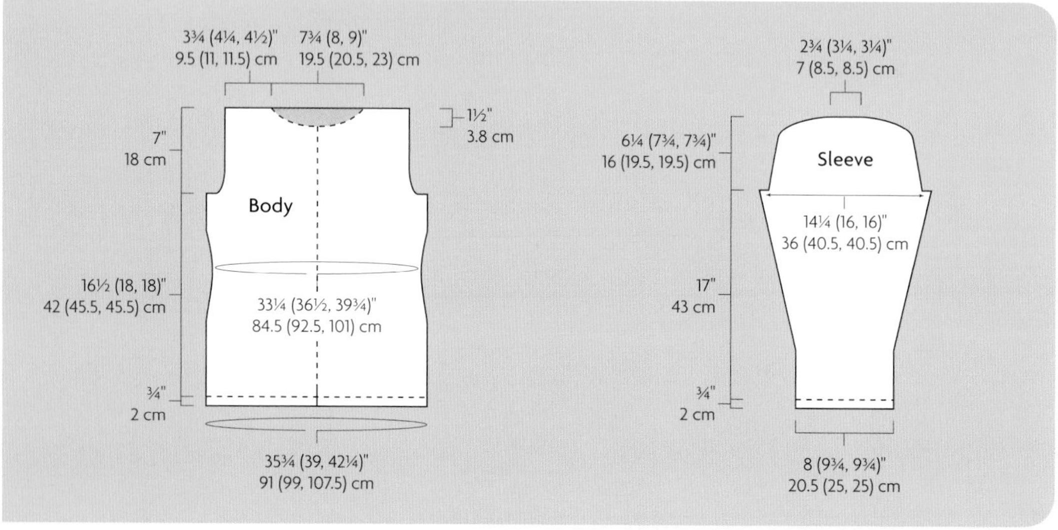
3¾ (4¼, 4½)"
9.5 (11, 11.5) cm
7¾ (8, 9)"
19.5 (20.5, 23) cm
1½"
3.8 cm
7"
18 cm
Body
16½ (18, 18)"
42 (45.5, 45.5) cm
33¼ (36½, 39¾)"
84.5 (92.5, 101) cm
¾"
2 cm
35¾ (39, 42¼)"
91 (99, 107.5) cm
2¾ (3¼, 3¼)"
7 (8.5, 8.5) cm
6¼ (7¾, 7¾)"
16 (19.5, 19.5) cm
Sleeve
14¼ (16, 16)"
36 (40.5, 40.5) cm
17"
43 cm
¾"
2 cm
8 (9¾, 9¾)"
20.5 (25, 25) cm

STITCH GUIDE

Picot Cast-On
Using the cable method (see Glossary), *CO 5 sts, BO 3 sts; rep from * for the desired number of sts.

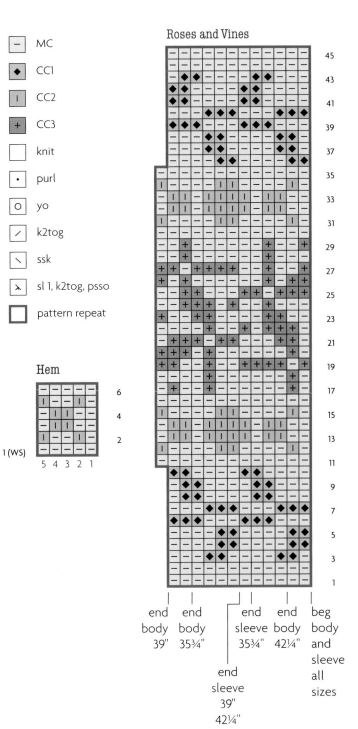

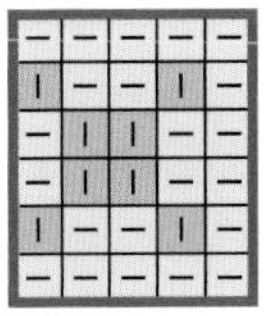

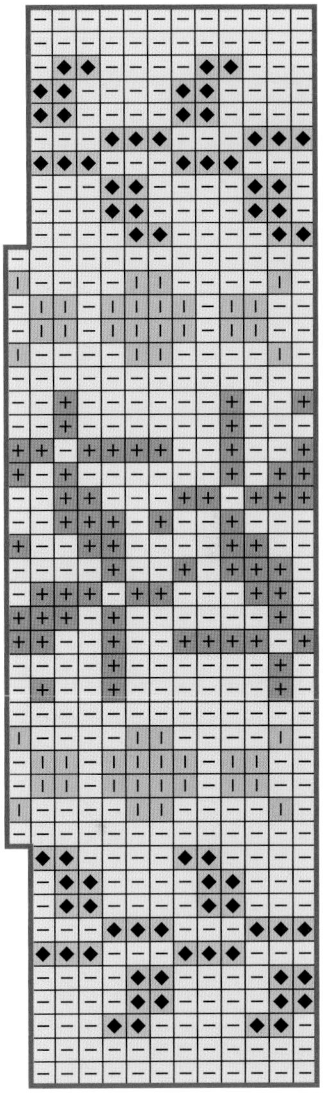

BODY

With MC and smallest cir needle, CO 286 (312, 338) sts. Do not join. Work back and forth in St st for 6 rows. Change to CC1 and knit 1 row. **Picot row:** (WS) *K2tog, yo; rep from * to last 2 sts, k2tog—1 st dec'd. Change to middle-size cir needle and knit 1 row, inc 1 st at beg of row—1 st inc'd. Beg with a WS row and the 1st (2nd, 3rd) st of the chart, work Rows 1–6 of Hem chart. **Joining rnd:** Place marker (pm), use the backward-loop method (see Glossary) to CO 6 sts for center front steek (see page 124; these sts are not included in st counts unless otherwise indicated), pm, and join for working in rnds, being careful not to twist sts. Beg and end as indicated for your size, work Rows 1–45 of Roses and Vines chart, placing markers to denote side "seams" as foll: Work 70 (78, 84) sts for right front, pm, work 146 (156, 170) sts for back, pm, work 70 (78, 84) sts for left front. **Note:** On Rows 11–35 of Roses and Vines chart, beg with the first st and end with the last st of the chart. Rep Rows 1–24 of Rosebud chart (see page 96) and *at the same time* beg with Row 6, shape waist as foll: **Dec rnd:** Keeping in patt, *work to 4 sts before side m, k2tog, k2, slip marker (sl m), k2, ssk; rep from * once more, work to end of rnd—4 sts dec'd. Work 5 rnds even in patt. Rep the shaping of the last 6 rnds 4 more times—266 (292, 318) sts rem. Work 11 rnds even in patt. **Inc rnd:** *Work to 2 sts before side m, M1R (see Glossary), k2, sl m, k2, M1L (see Glossary); rep from * once more, work to end of rnd—4 sts inc'd. Work 5 rnds even in patt. Rep the shaping of the last 6 rnds 4 more times, working new sts into patt—286 (312, 338) sts. Work even in patt until piece measures 16½ (18, 18)" (42 [45.5, 45.5] cm) from picot row.

–	MC
◆	CC1
I	CC2
+	CC3
☐	knit
·	purl
o	yo
/	k2tog
\	ssk
⅄	sl 1, k2tog, psso
☐	pattern repeat

Roses and Vines

Hem

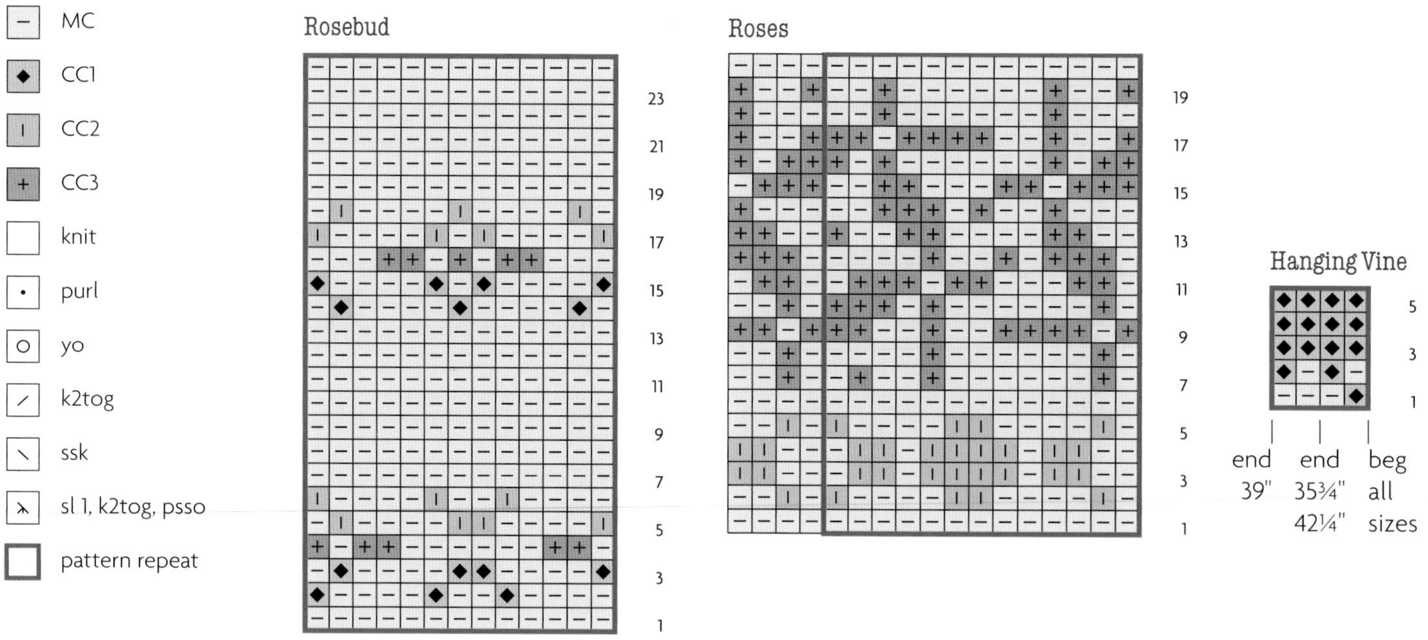

Shape Armholes

Keeping in patt, k64 (72, 78) for right front, BO 12 sts for right armhole, k134 (144, 158) for back, BO 12 sts for left armhole, k64 (72, 78) for left front. **Next rnd:** K60 (68, 74), k2tog, k2, pm, use the backward-loop method to CO 6 sts for right armhole steek (these sts are not included in st counts unless otherwise indicated), pm, k2, ssk, k126 (136, 150), k2tog, k2, pm, use the backward-loop method to CO 6 sts for left armhole steek, pm, k2, ssk, k60 (68, 74)—63 (71, 77) sts rem for each front, 132 (142, 156) sts rem for back. Work 1 rnd even. **Dec rnd:** *Work to 4 sts before side m, k2tog, k2, work 6 steek sts, k2, ssk; rep from * once more, work to end of rnd—4 sts dec'd. Rep dec rnd every other rnd 4 more times—58 (66, 72) sts rem for each front, 122 (132, 146) sts rem for back. Work even until piece measures about 20¾ (22¼, 22¼)" (52.5 [56.5, 56.5] cm) from picot row, ending with Row 6 or 18 of chart. Work Rows 1–20 of Roses chart. Beg and end as indicated for your size, work Rows 1–5 of Hanging Vine chart.

Place Stitches on Holders

With CC1 and beg at center of front steek, BO 3 steek sts, k28 (32, 35) and place these sts on holder for right front neck, k30 (34, 37) and place these sts on a second holder for right front shoulder, BO 6 right armhole steek sts, k30 (34, 37) and place these sts on a third holder for right back shoulder, k62 (64, 72) and place these sts on a fourth holder for back neck, k30 (34, 37) and place these sts on a fifth holder for left back shoulder, BO 6 left armhole steek sts, k30 (34, 37) and place these sts on a sixth holder for left front shoulder, k28 (32, 35) and place these sts on a seventh holder for left front neck, BO rem 3 steek sts.

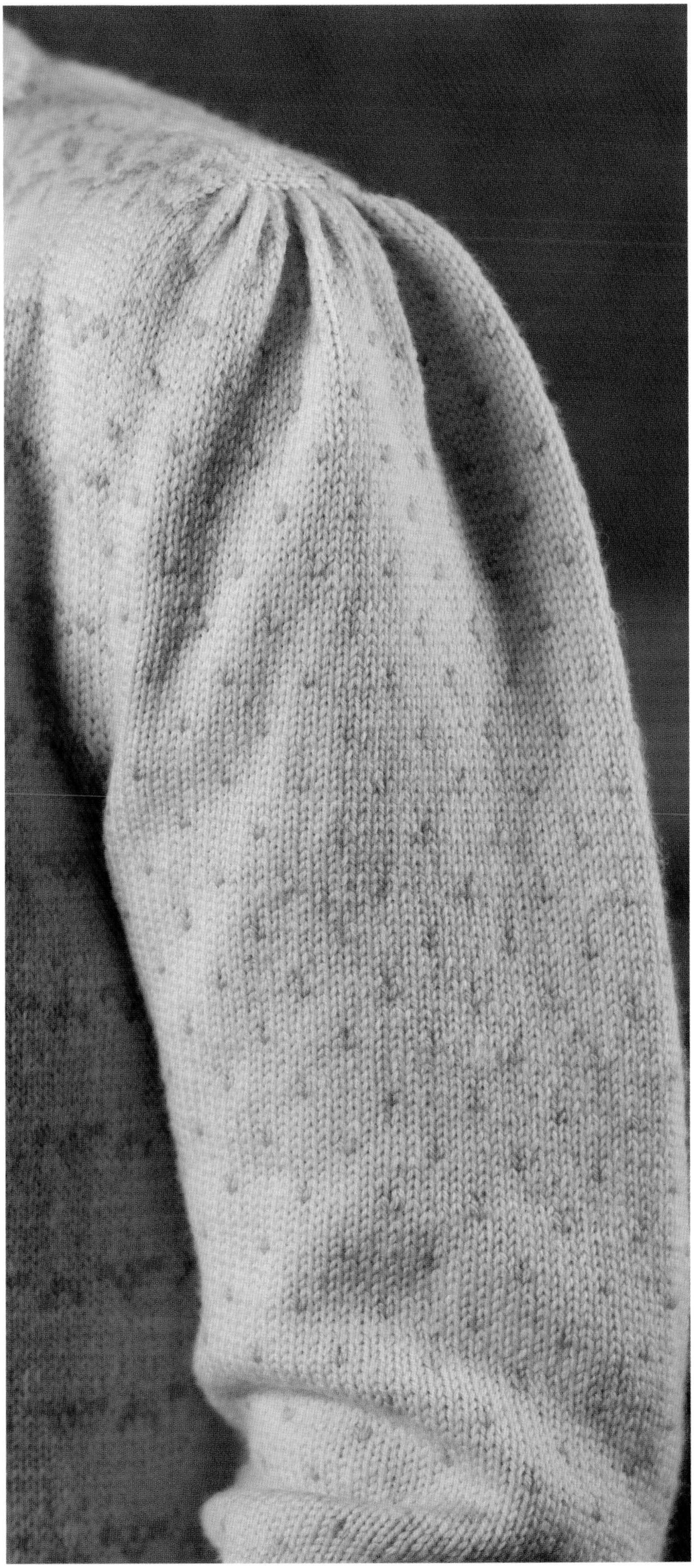

Lice (pronounced "leese" in Norwegian): A small one-stitch motif against a contrasting background. The origin of the term is oblique, but it may be related to the tendency of knitters to pick at these stitches when they appear uneven. When working lice, work the background stitch following the lice stitch a bit more snugly than its neighbors to coax the stitch to "pop forward." To prevent stretching the single-stitch lice on the following row, work the stitch at the narrow tips of the needle.

Lace

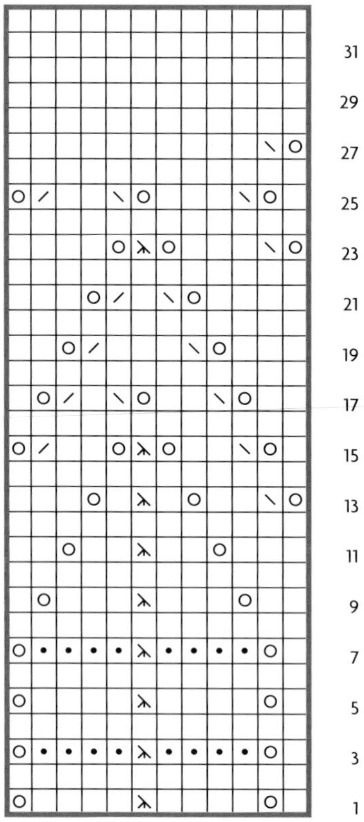

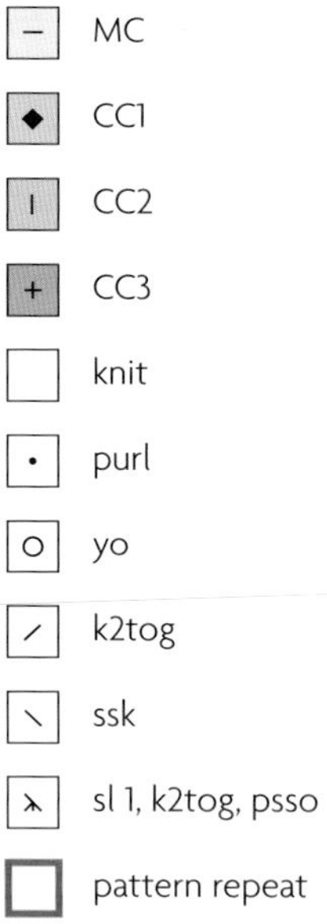

Sleeve

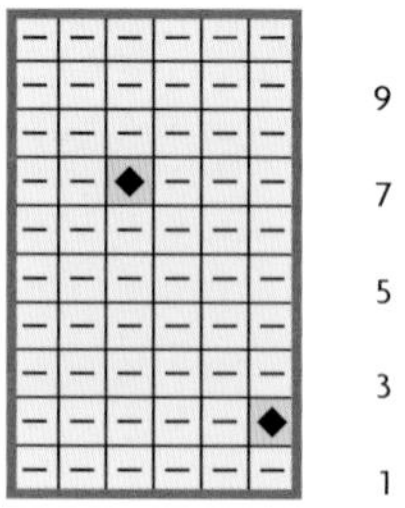

LACE CUFF (make 2)

With MC, smallest needle, and using the picot method (see Stitch Guide on page 95), CO 84 sts. Arrange sts as evenly as possible on 3 or 4 dpn, pm, and join for working in rnds, being careful not to twist sts. Change to largest dpn. *K2tog, yo; rep from * to end of rnd. Work Rows 1–32 of Lace chart. Loosely BO all sts.

SLEEVES (make 2)

With MC and smallest needle, CO 66 (78, 78) sts. Do not join. Work back and forth in St st for 6 rows. With CC1, knit 1 RS row. **Picot row:** (WS) *K2tog, yo; rep from * to last 2 sts, k2tog—1 st dec'd. Change to middle-size cir needle and knit 1 row, inc 0 (1, 1) st at beg of row—65 (78, 78) sts. Beg with a WS row and with the 5th (3rd, 3rd) st of chart, work Rows 1–6 of Hem chart (see page 95). Arrange sts as evenly as possible on 3 or 4 dpn, pm, and join for working in rnds, being careful not to twist sts. Beg and end as indicated for your size, work Rows 1–34 of Roses and Vines chart. **Note:** On Rows 11–35 of Roses and Vines chart, beg with the first st and end with the last st of the chart. **Next rnd:** (Row 35 of chart) Keeping in patt, inc 1 st each end of rnd—2 sts inc'd. Cont in patt, work 4 rnds even. Rep the shaping of the last 5 rnds 24 more times and *at the same time* work through Row 45 of Roses and Vines chart, then rep Rows 1–10 of Sleeve chart until shaping is complete—115 (128, 128) sts; piece measures about 17" (43 cm) from picot row.

Shape Cap

Keeping in patt, place last 6 sts worked onto a holder, k6, then place these 6 sts onto the same holder, knit to end—103 (116, 116) sts rem. Working back and forth in rows, purl 1 (WS) row. **Dec row:** (RS) K2, ssk, knit to last 4 sts, k2tog, k2—2 sts dec'd. Work 1 row even. Rep the last 2 rows 5 more times—91 (104, 104) sts rem. Work even in patt until piece measures 23 (24½, 24½)" (58.5 [62, 62] cm) from picot row, ending with a WS row.

Gather Top

With MC, [k4tog] 11 (13, 13) times, [k3tog] 1 (0, 0) time, [k4tog] 11 (13, 13) times—23 (26, 26) sts rem. Purl 1 row.

Facing

K23 (26, 26), pick up and knit 50 (62, 62) sts along edge of cap, pm, k12 held armhole sts, pm, pick up and knit 50 (62, 62) sts along other edge of cap—135 (162, 162) sts total. Pm and join for working in rnds. Turn piece inside out so WS faces outward (purl side of facing will show on RS of sleeve). **Inc rnd:** Knit to first m, M1R, sl m, k12, sl m, M1L, knit to end of rnd—2 sts inc'd. Rep inc rnd every rnd 5 more times—147 (174, 174) sts. BO all sts.

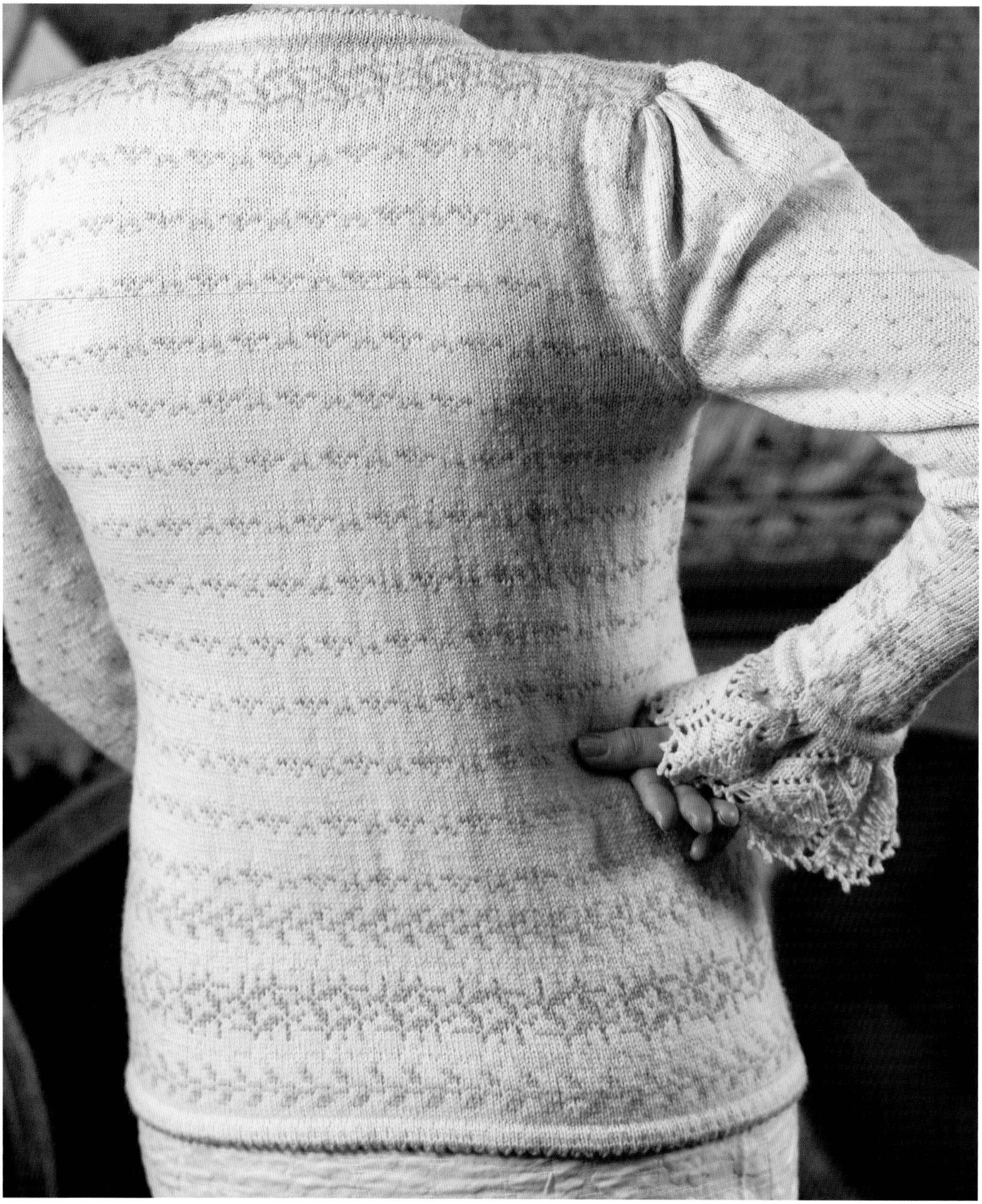

Block pieces that contain a lot of lice with the wrong side facing up so that the floats will not create horizontal ridges in the work as it dries flat.

FINISHING

Weave in loose ends. Block pieces to measurements.

Steeks

Machine stitch and cut center front and armhole steeks as described on pages 125–127. Mark, machine stitch, and cut front neckline curve to a depth of 1½" (3.8 cm) as described on page 129. Fold lower body and sleeve facings to WS along picot row and, with sharp-point sewing needle and matching thread, sew in place as invisibly as possible.

Join Shoulders

Place 30 (34, 37) held right front shoulder sts on one needle and the corresponding 30 (34, 37) held right back shoulder sts on another needle. With RS tog, use the three-needle method as described on page 130 to BO the shoulder sts tog. Rep for other shoulder.

Neck Binding

With MC, middle-size cir needle, and RS facing, pick up and knit 32 (34, 38) sts evenly spaced along right front neck edge, k62 (64, 72) held back neck sts, pick up and knit 32 (34, 38) sts evenly spaced along left front neck edge—126 (132, 148) sts total. Working back and forth in rows and beg with st 1 (2, 3) of chart, work Rows 1–6 of Hem chart. With CC1, purl 1 WS row. **Picot row:** (RS) *K2tog, yo; rep from * to last 2 sts, k2tog—1 st dec'd. Change to smallest needle and purl 1 row. With MC, work 6 rows in St st for facing. Loosely BO all sts. Turn facing to WS along picot row and, with sharp-point sewing needle and matching thread, sew in place as invisibly as possible.

Front Binding

With MC, middle-size cir needle, and RS facing, pick up and knit 160 (172, 172) sts evenly spaced along right front edge between steek and body sts. Beg with st 5 (2, 2) of chart, work Rows 1–6 of Hem chart. Work WS row, picot row, and facing as for neck binding. Loosely BO all sts. Turn facing to WS along picot row and sew in place as for neck binding. Rep for left front edge.

Apply optional ribbon/trim along side of front bands, placing ⅜" (1 cm) wide ribbon next to band, 1¾" (4.5 cm) wide ribbon next to ⅜" (1 cm) ribbon, and ½" (1.3 cm) wide ribbon next to 1¾" (4.5 cm) ribbon. Sew clasps to front, placing the highest just below the upper edge of the front binding, the lowest 6" (15 cm) above the lower edge, and the others evenly spaced between. Gather top edge of lace cuffs and, with sharp-point sewing needle and matching thread, sew RS of lace cuffs to WS of lower sleeves along CO edges of sleeve hems. With MC threaded on a tapestry needle, sew sleeve caps into armholes as described on page 132, matching centers of sleeves to shoulder seams. Fold sleeve facings to WS to cover cut edges of armhole steeks and sew in place.

stranded colorwork techniques

There are only a few special things to know about knitting in color. Just as in music there are only so many notes, in knitting, the basic elements are always the same: needles, yarn, and persistence.

My knowledge comes by way of dumb luck, reckless experimentation, standing on the shoulders of geniuses, and sometimes all three. This is my little collection of favorite colorwork techniques: some obvious, some obscure, very few original. What makes it special is that it's all in one place, and it's all about stranded colorwork.

I hope this information will help you to execute both my designs, and your own.

STICKS AND STRINGS

As with other forms of knitting, you will favor certain tools for stranded colorwork. New gadgets and gizmos are invented every day to make our knitting faster, braver, and stronger. Some of them even work, too. My advice is to try every new thing that intrigues you, with the sure conviction that the only items that are absolutely necessary to the process are yarn, needles, and a positive attitude. Just as I would consider myself unqualified to advise you in the purchase of your next toothbrush, I won't presume to give you specifics on knitting tools. Your favorite tools are a matter of personal choice. For every knitter who insists that stiletto-pointed needles are the only way to go, there is another who maintains they'll put your eye out. Your preferences may evolve—the stitch holders I prefer today would have made me miserable a couple of years ago. I am a work in progress and so are my knitting tools.

That said, I will recommend a few useful things that can make knitting more fun. Without exception, I encourage you to acquire the very best tools you can afford. Your work will reflect the quality of what was used to create it, so don't scrimp on the good stuff. You have my permission to both elevate and validate the importance of your knitting by getting yourself some really supreme gear.

Yarn

Once, a foolhardy but well-intentioned soul (okay, it was my spouse) suggested that I had "enough" yarn. " 'Enough?' " I asked incredulously. "Do you suppose that people used to tell van Gogh that he had 'enough' paint? Did Eiffel have 'enough' steel girders? Do you think Noah had 'enough' animal species?" No, my friends, there is no such thing. There are only minimum stock levels that must be maintained. I would like to be able to say that it was the last conversation I had with my husband on the subject of yarn inventory, but alas, I cannot. He still labors under the delusion that someday I will actually reach critical yarn mass and stop stockpiling. Poor dear.

I have learned from my own trials that there are a few things that deserve consideration when choosing yarn for a colorwork project. These are frequently the same elements that inspire me in the first place. I am not the knitter to tell anyone that they must always or never do, or not do, anything. If you have the fortitude to try, the sky's the limit for your experiments.

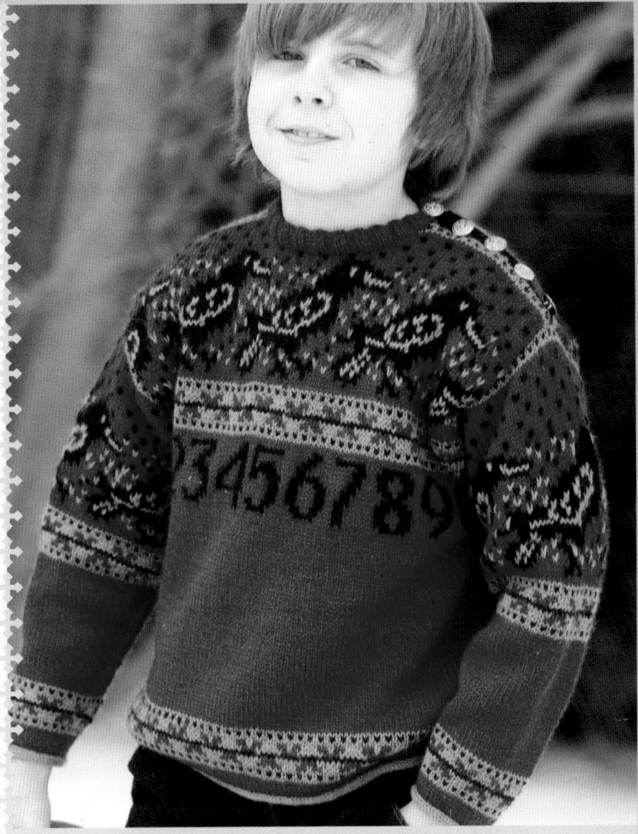

If you use color-change, variegated, or self-striping yarn for one or more of the strands in your work, knit the two sleeves simultaneously with steeks so that the color progression will be the same on each sleeve.

Don't have matching thread? Use a single ply of yarn to sew on buttons or hooks.

Fiber

Any type of yarn can be used for stranded colorwork, but some fibers are friendlier than others, especially when you're first starting. Wool is without a doubt the most elastic, most cooperative, most forgiving option. Within that category, you can choose from untreated, superwash, and blends (all are featured in this book), each of which has its own advantages. If you really and truly do not wish to work with wool, there are more options available to you now than ever, and I encourage you to experiment with an open mind.

Texture

An important quality of any fiber is its ability to stick to itself. Cotton and bast fibers, which tend to slide rather than stick, are less ideal than wool and other animal fibers (and their blends), which are stickier. Traditional stranded knitting construction techniques rely on this bonding property: the more adhesive or feltable the fiber you choose, the easier your work will be and the more reliable the results. Another consideration is stitch definition. Broadly speaking, smooth, uniform yarns show charted motifs to better advantage than fluffy, bumpy, or irregular ones.

Weight

With one exception (the felted Go For Baroque bag on page 30), all of the projects in this collection call for yarn that is classified as DK weight or lighter. The reason is simple: more than one strand is used at a time. Heavier-weight yarns can make for bulky and over-insulating garments. Modern buildings feature central heating systems, unlike the dwellings of the early practitioners of stranded knitting. Fine-gauge yarn is your friend.

Color

Color is the driving force behind most of my design choices. If I find just the shade of Granny Smith apple green that I have in mind, other considerations will be made after I've counted how many skeins are available. Besides the hue, I consider the feel of the project and how the color choices can support the theme. For example, the yarn I chose for Being Koi (page 20) is complicated and multifaceted to mimic the sense of looking through water. The yarn I chose for Houndstooth (page 46) has a straightforward, matte look, perfect for the naïve folk-art quality I was after.

Have a great time picking out the yarns you like best for your project, using your own level of joy in the selection as your guide. Remember that if you dislike a color at the beginning of a project, you're unlikely to like it any better at the end. Feel free to reject any yarn that doesn't delight you—only yarn you love deserves to be in your knitting.

Needles

Most of the projects in this book call for two sizes of circular needles—one short (16" [40 cm]) and one long (24" to 32" [60 to 80 cm]). Collect the super-expensive can't-live-without-them favorites of your choice (one set at a time, if need be). Your wrists, elbows, and mental health are all at stake here. Tell your family it's for their protection, too, that you need to splurge on the best.

Other Necessities

Stitch Markers

You'll want eight or ten markers in different colors (a dozen isn't too many). I like the pretty little ones made out of jewelry findings and beads because they are easier to spot when I drop them on the floor, sofa, or ferry-boat deck. The kind that resembles safety pins is also nice for marking rows. Whatever style you choose, it's a good idea to have a variety of sizes to accommodate different needle sizes and yarn weights. Fine-gauge yarn and needles call for small markers; markers that are too big can create visual vertical ridges in the knitting.

Keep a notepad handy to keep track of any changes you make to a pattern. This will be extremely helpful should you elect to knit the pattern again (or if you decide to make a second sleeve).

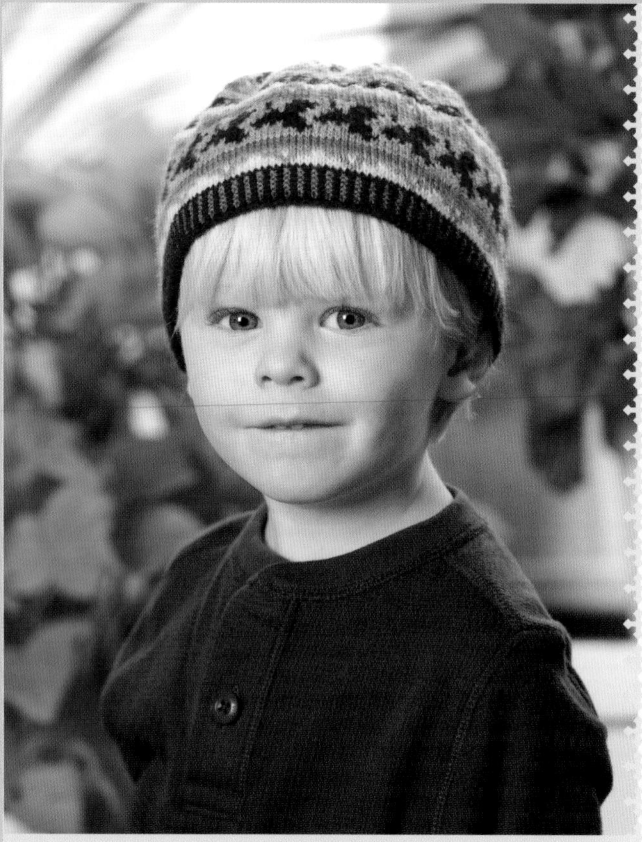

Concerned about choosing compatible colors? Select yarn that has been dyed with natural dyestuffs. Colors that originate in nature never "clash."

Tapestry Needle
Make sure this is a blunt-tipped needle with a large eye that's easy to thread with yarn. When you find a size or brand you like, go crazy and buy a stockpile. Tapestry needles disappear in inverse proportion to the availability of replacements.

Waste Yarn or Stitch Holders
If you prefer using stitch holders to waste yarn, you will need a lot of them. Seven or eight stitch holders are common for a full-size sweater. Smooth cotton waste yarn won't stick or leave lint behind and goes easily under the presser foot of your sewing machine.

Shears
Never, ever, ever, on pain of torture at the hands of the knitting gods, use dull, bent, or otherwise sub-standard scissors on your knitting. Get a decent pair of 8" (20.5 cm) sewing shears and hide them from all other members of your household. Trust me on this: You do not want to cut a steek using shears that have been used in household wiring or barbed-wire fencing schemes. Enough said.

Sewing Machine
Although steeks can be secured by hand sewing or crochet, this book describes machine-sewing technique.

You will need a working sewing machine in good repair for stitching steeks. The machine does not need to be fancy; it only has to stitch a straight line. Thread tension, stitch length, and balance problems should all be addressed before you bring your sweater near it. Use a new needle—either sharp or universal rather than ball-pointed—and thread that contrasts sharply with the main color of the yarn (white or black is fine). Don't worry, it won't show in the end.

CONSTRUCTION: OF CARPENTRY AND PLUMBING

Okay, I'll admit it's an unexpected metaphor, but stay with me and I promise to make sense. More scholarly knitters than I have suggested that knitting in the round predates knitting flat (back and forth in rows). They assert that the earliest knitters devised the way to make tubes with their string, then some other clever souls figured out how to make a flat fabric. Most modern knitters teach each other how to create stockinette stitch the other way around: First we learn how to make flat pieces, then we graduate to going around in circles. This is counterintuitive in my opinion—producing stockinette stitch circularly requires mastery of just the knit stitch, to work it back and forth we must know how to purl as well.

Think of knitted construction like this: If you are a carpenter using pieces of wood, making the flat pieces into something useful will require you to shape them by lopping off bits of them to give them shape. While the desired useful object will exist in three dimensions, the materials used and the planning process to get there will mostly use only two. Carpentry is flat. Now, if you are a plumber trying to move various substances (usually wet) from one place to another, you will need tubes. Getting the wet stuff to change direction will require you to make intersections between one tube and another. This is a three-dimensional concept, and planning for it will make you think that way.

I'm not implying that carpenters are better than plumbers, or vice versa. Both are useful and necessary contributions to modern society, and I wouldn't want to get along without either one. I merely wish to illustrate the fundamental differences in engineering and entice you to think about your knitting in a new way.

When working sleeves in the round, close the bottom of the tube with a covered elastic ponytail holder and drop the balls of yarn inside to prevent them from rolling around free range while you knit.

The traditional definition of a steek is an area of extra "waste" stitches that are designated to be cut later. For the purposes of this book, I've expanded this definition to include all areas of knitting that are marked, reinforced, and cut, regardless of whether or not they include extra "waste" stitches.

Now, add color to the construction process. In stranded color knitting, we make patterns by using more than one color of yarn in a row, following a charted pattern. It's much easier to follow the charted pattern when looking at the public, or knit, side of the work. Working back and forth in rows necessitates following the rows on the chart first one direction (from right to left on right-side rows), then the other (from left to right on wrong-side rows). Things get even more complicated because the wrong-side rows must be purled instead of knitted. I like a challenge as much as the next guy—maybe more—but I would much rather work my stranded knitting in just one direction with one type of stitch. Plenty of patterns have been written or edited by people who either didn't feel this way or didn't understand. I suspect that stranded color knitting has suffered greatly in terms of popularity due to this problem. If you survived to the end of a flat-knitted colorwork sweater with shaping and seams, you might not attempt a second one.

When we knit flat, we work like carpenters to make two-dimensional shaped pieces that are then seamed together into three-dimensional forms that fit our bodies. When we knit circularly, we work like plumbers, forming tubes that connect to one another. We just knit some tubes and cut away waste wherever necessary to connect them. It could be said that stranded color knitting makes pipe fitters of us all. Of course, our work is much more fun than carpentry or plumbing because we get to do it with yarn.

CHARTED TERRITORY

There are many ways to color your knitting. Intarsia, Fair Isle, and Norwegian are just a few of the cunning techniques that knitters have devised over the centuries to keep things interesting (and warm) for themselves and their loved ones. I enthusiastically encourage you to sample all you can find on the subject. Much has been written and even more invented. Your personal contribution to the tradition of color knitting will be its freshest breath of air and your innovations will keep it alive and vital for future generations.

There are important differences between the styles of colorwork, and it would be a mistake to use the terms interchangeably.

Intarsia is made by working areas or blocks of color that differ from the background. A separate bobbin (a separate length or "mini" ball of yarn) is used for each area of color. Intarsia patterns can involve a dozen or more bobbins in a single row. The bobbins must be twisted around one another at color changes to prevent holes from forming.

Fair Isle is achieved by using two or more balls of yarn in the same round of knitting. The color that is not being worked is stranded across the back (non-public side) of the work. The strands are caught at regular intervals to prevent long floats of unused yarn. Special attention is given in the design of Fair Isle motifs to ensure that one color does not travel behind another for more than five or six stitches. The motifs themselves are also special in that they are specific to their place of origin.

Closures look better in uneven numbers. Sets of two or three small buttons are an interesting alternative to a single large button.

To create sharper picots for a turning row, purl two stitches together instead of knitting two stitches together.

Norwegian knitting calls for two colors (rarely more) per row. Like Fair Isle, Norwegian knitting employs the stranded technique of carrying the color not in use on the non-public side of the work. The important distinction is that the yarns are *not* caught around each other unless absolutely necessary and there is no guideline regarding how many stitches may be between color changes. The motifs in traditional Norwegian knitting are often also region specific.

The patterns in this book are designed to use the Norwegian technique. Referring to it as "Norwegian," though, is probably unfair to the many other cultures which have embraced and enhanced it. Instead, I like to call it "stranded colorwork."

After choosing yarn and tools, you'll need a pattern, which for stranded colorwork will include one or more charts. You can follow the patterns and charts in this book to the letter, or you can use them as springboards for your own designs. The motifs for many of the projects in this book are based on the same number of stitches in a repeat, making them easily interchangeable. For example, Johnny Jump Up (page 64) and Leafy Toque (page 6) both use charts with nine-stitch motif repeats.

Reading Charts

All charts in this book are read from right to left and from bottom to top, row by row. For some rows, you need only glance at the chart to know what to do—the colors in one row connect logically and organically to the row(s) below. Other rows will appear less logical or symmetrical and will require more attention. Be patient and read each one carefully. These "complicated" rows are necessary for truly unusual designs. To make it easier to keep your place in a chart, cover the upper part of the chart—everything above the row you're working on—with a piece of paper or sticky note. For large charts, I like to laminate color copies, then use painters' masking tape (available at hardware stores) to mark the row I'm working. This trick has the added advantage of protecting my knitting books since I don't have to haul them around in my knitting bag. A laminated copy is also much lighter and more durable (though less aerodynamic when thrown in frustration).

Centering Motifs

Some pattern instructions will call for you to center a motif where increases, decreases, or size differences make the stitch count unclear. To center a motif, use a stitch marker to denote the center of the piece. The center will be between two stitches if there is an even number of stitches; it will be in the center of stitch if there is an odd number of stitches, in which case the marker should be placed to the left of the center stitch. Then count backward to the beginning of the row in multiples of the motif repeat to determine which box of the chart corresponds to the first stitch on the needles. Centering a motif will often cause the first and last motifs to be incomplete, but these partial repeats are engineered to fall where they will be less visible, such as the underarm.

Adding a Third Color

There are some designs in which I simply could not resist adding a third color to certain rows. There are three ways to deal with this additional color.

- Ignore my lack of self-control and work these stitches in one of the two working colors used for that row. Life is complicated enough without three-color rows, for pity's sake, and I won't hold it against you.
- Carry a third strand of yarn behind the work, tacking the floats wherever you deem necessary (more on float-tacking on page 118). Feel free to both curse the evil designer and congratulate yourself on your dexterity as you execute this plan.
- Work these stitches in one of the two working colors used for that row, then when the knitting is finished, add the third color with duplicate stitches (see Glossary), referring back to the chart for placement. I sometimes even make little French knots (see Glossary) when I do this, which I'll indicate in the instructions.

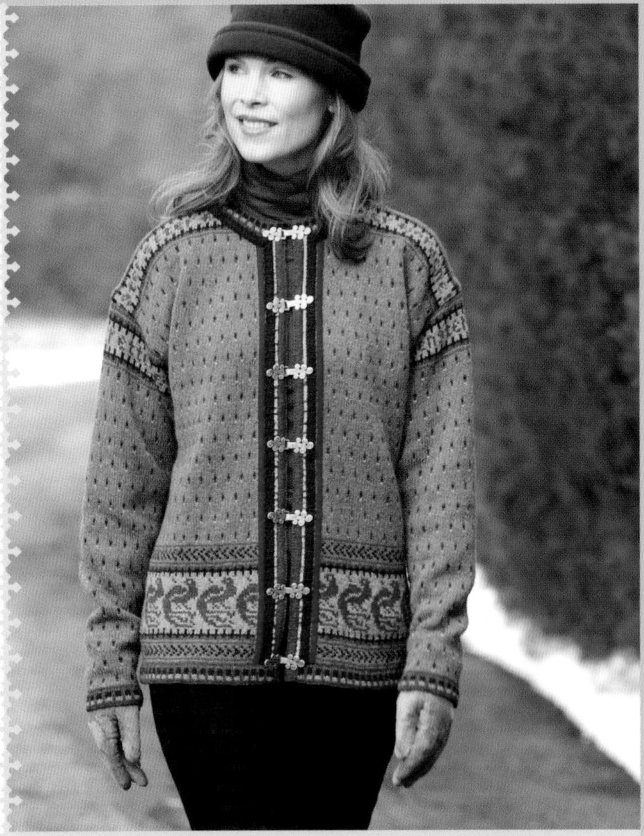

Change to a larger diameter needle (two sizes larger) when knitting in hems to eliminate a horizontal ridge where the fabric changes from double thickness to single thickness.

When seaming with very fine yarn (such as 2-ply Shetland), double the yarn to strengthen it and prevent breakage as you sew.

KNOTS AND TAILS

By the time most knitters are ready to take on stranded colorwork, they have come to espouse a particular position about the tying of knots. They usually fall into two camps—knot-tiers and non-knot-tiers. While it is not my intention to convert anyone from their own hard-won conviction, I confess to being a knot-tier. I do not tie knots if I can spit-splice (see at right) the end of one ball of yarn with the beginning of another. All other times, for me, there will be knots. The knots have to follow certain rules, however, or they don't make it into my knitting:

- Knots must be adjacent to or inside a steek.
- Knots are only made when changing from one color to a different color.
- Knots must be of the weaver's or overhand variety (see page 114).

I sometimes break my own rules. For example, I tie knots in mittens, which have no steeks but many color changes. If you haven't figured it out already, you will when you see the construction in action: Color changes that are adjacent to steeks do not require the weaving in of yarn tails. That is why it's sometimes preferable to knit two sleeves simultaneously with steeks—the many yarn tails are more easily hidden as a group under a facing than woven in individually.

Knot-Tying Decision Matrix

SPIT-SPLICE	TIE KNOT AT STEEK
Same color, new skein	Color change
	Same color, superwash wool

Spit-Splice

Do not be put off by the name of this technique: knitters cannot afford to be faint of heart. If I can confidently ask you to cut up your knitting with scissors, I certainly can get away with telling you to spit on your yarn. The only caveat for spit-splicing is that you must use untreated 100% wool yarn—cotton, silk, microfiber, and even superwash wool will disappoint you here.

Separate the plies for about 2" (5 cm) from the end of the old ball of yarn and break off half of the plies **(Figure 1)**. Do the same to the first 2" (5 cm) of the new ball of yarn. Now comes the earthy part—put the ends of both strands in your mouth and get them really soggy. No, you cannot use water for this. No, you cannot daintily moisten your finger and apply the spit that way. Just suck it up (literally) until both strands are good and wet (this can take several seconds, so don't rush it, however fuzzy your tongue may feel). Remove the strand from your mouth and take a moment to delicately remove any residual tongue fuzz. Yes, this is gross, but we have already established that knitting is not for weenies. Next, lay the wet yarn ends on your palm, overlapping the wet ends **(Figure 2)**. Use your other palm to roll the strands together as if to make a clay snake, but more vigorously to create both heat and friction **(Figure 3)**. This agitation, combined with the enzymes in your saliva, creates the perfect felt right there in your hands.

When you are finished, the graft will be nearly dry, invisible, and even stronger than the rest of the yarn. Not a bad trade for getting a bit of fuzz in your mouth. One last note: I would advise against performing this maneuver in view of non-knitters. I wouldn't want you to have to explain yourself or your enzymes to anyone who wouldn't adequately appreciate the information.

Figure 1

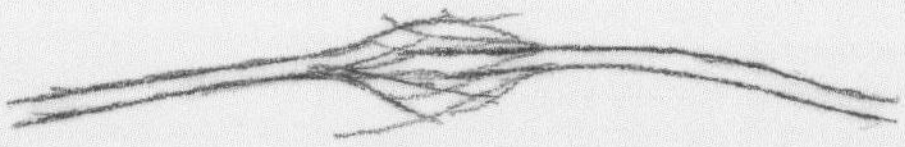

Figure 2

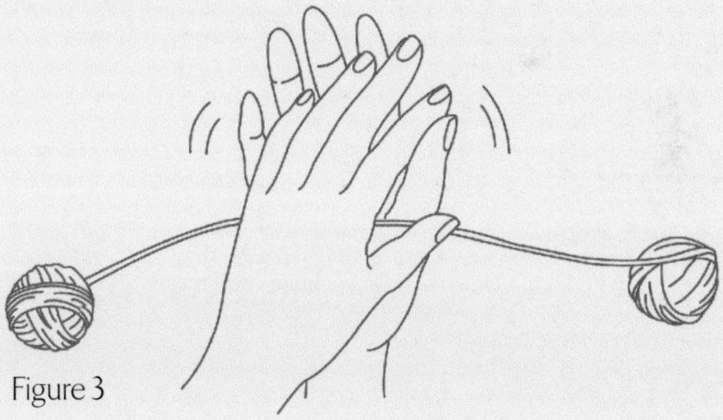

Figure 3

Weaver's Knot

Place the loose end of the new yarn (B; shown as dark) over the top of the old yarn (A; shown as light) to form an "X" **(Figure 1)**. Bring the loose end of A over the top of B, back under A, and over B again to form a loop **(Figure 2)**. Bring the loose end of B down through the loop formed by A **(Figure 3)**. Pull on both loose ends to tighten the knot **(Figure 4)**.

Figure 1

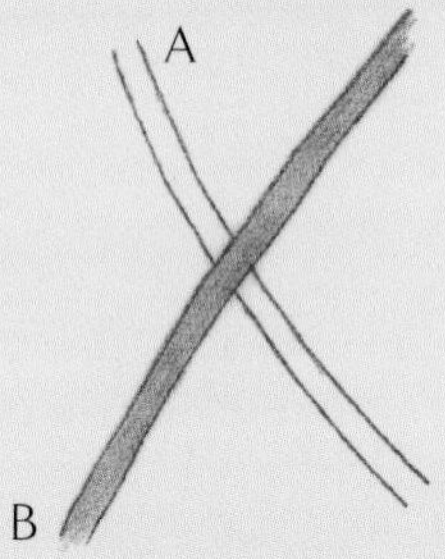

Figure 2

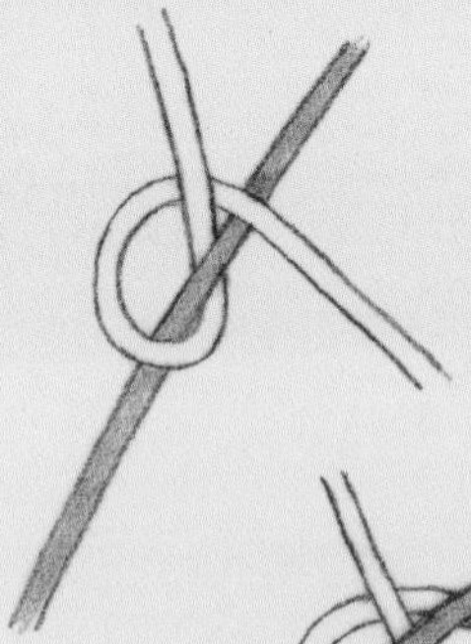

Figure 3

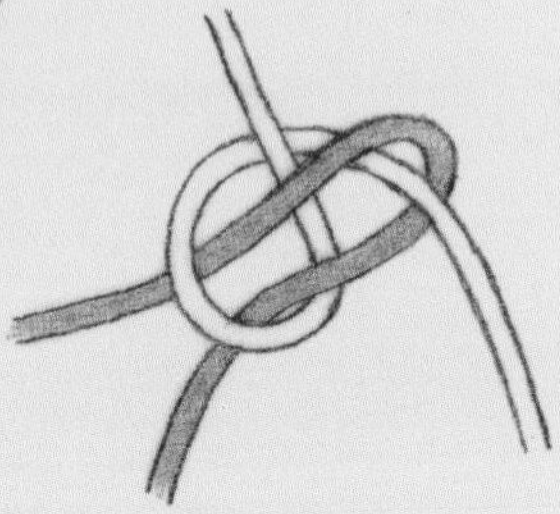

Figure 4

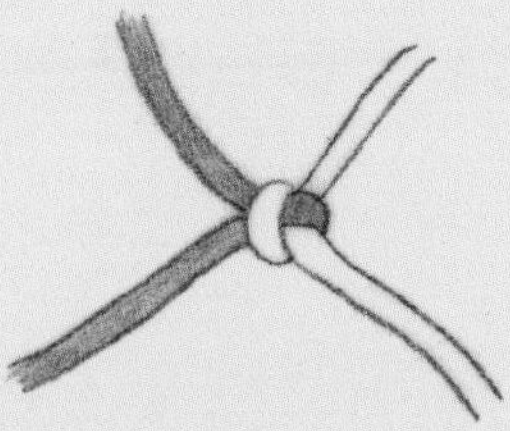

CARRY ON

Stranded colorwork knitting involves using (and tensioning) two strands of yarn in a single row of knitting. How you achieve this is, and should be, a personal choice. Rather than tell you what you should or should not do, I will here dispel some myths that crop up when knitters talk amongst themselves on the subject. After that I will illuminate the two mechanical concepts you actually need.

Color Knitting Myth #1
You have to be able to carry one or more of the working strands in your left hand (Continental style) in order to knit stranded colorwork.

Fact: This misunderstanding is probably rooted in the fact that the traditions of stranded colorwork originated in countries outside America. Some knitters in these places hold the working yarn in their left hand. To make stranded color knitting, you only have to knit. How you do it is entirely your own choice.

Color Knitting Myth #2
You have to twist the yarn strands around each other to prevent holes from forming in the knitting.

Fact: This misinformation results from confusing the techniques of stranded color knitting, Fair Isle knitting, and intarsia. If you have read this far, you already know better.

Color Knitting Myth #3
Using more than one color at a time is complicated and hard to learn.

Fact: You would not believe how often people tell me this, even while I am sitting in front of them doing it. The fact that I could learn is testament to the very fallacy of this statement. The reality is that stranded color knitting looks much more complicated than it is.

There are only two things you need to know for stranded color knitting: how to alternate colors and how to regulate the tension of your work. That's it—two things. You can do this, and you really will have fun when you do.

Thing One

To alternate colors, you have to have two strands of yarn. You can hold them however you want, and you can change your mind as often as you wish to find the method that works best for you. After getting both colors attached to your work (tie a little knot, or don't, depending on your preference; see page 112), make a command decision about which strand will be the receding color (A) and which strand will be the dominant (B) one. Depending on the type of yarn, your tension, the relative humidity, and planetary alignment, your dominant color may or may not stick out a bit from the background of your receding color in the finished work. By "stick out," I mean that the stitch may physically protrude or raise up a bit from the rest of the knitting. This is a desirable trend, but don't worry about it too much if you don't see it happening. I only mention it because if you would rather refer to your two colors as background and foreground, that would be perfectly natural, too. What if the pattern you are working has no discernable background and foreground? That's why it's a command decision. What does matter is that you carry the strand you have labeled "A" (receding, background) above the strand you have labeled "B" (dominant, foreground) at all times. If you have to twist the two (more on that later), make sure to return them to their respective upper and lower positions. If you forget which is which, here's a simple trick: Always think of the darker color as "A" and the lighter color as "B". This will cause the lighter color to be dominant every time, but keeping the strands in the correct order is more important than which is dominant.

Overhand Knot

Holding the loose ends together, form a loop so that the loose ends cross over the top **(Figure 1)**. Bring the ends through the loop from back to front **(Figure 2)**. Pull on the ends to tighten **(Figure 3)**.

Figure 1

Figure 2

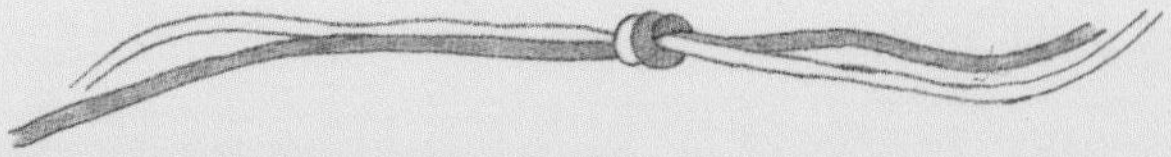

Figure 3

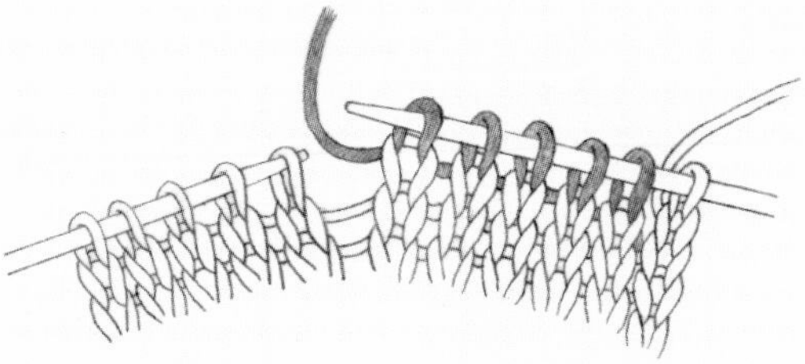

Figure 1

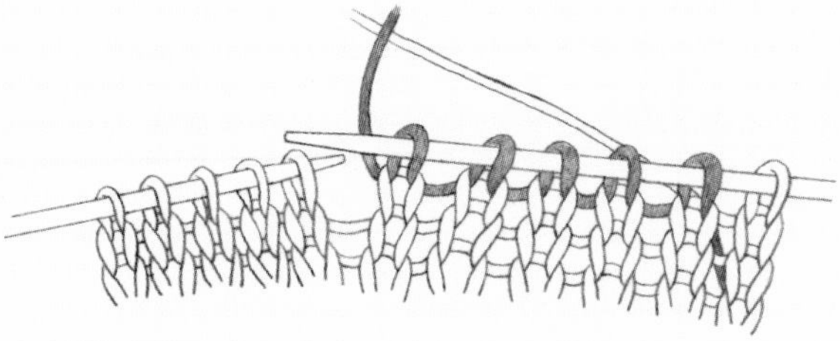

Figure 2

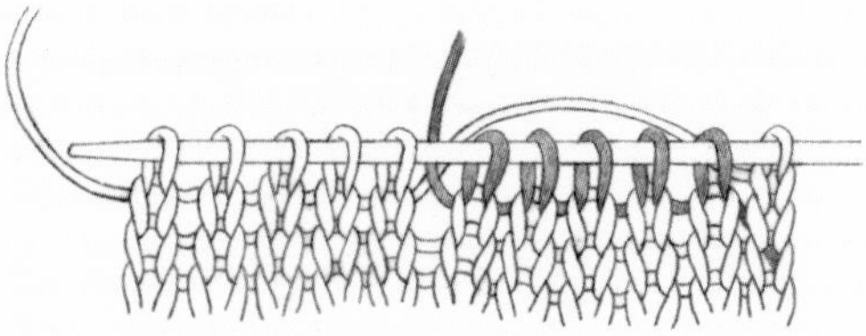

Figure 3

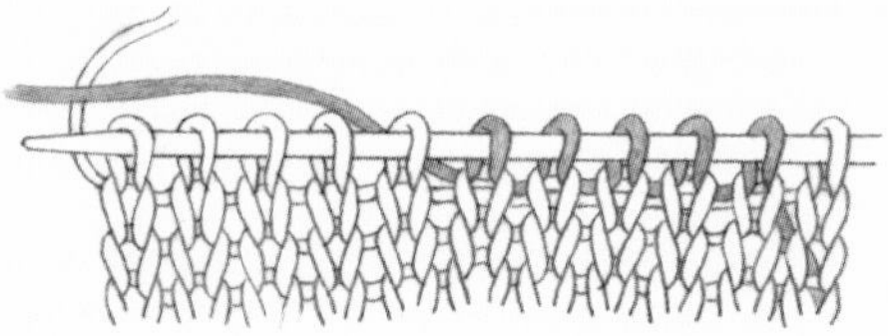

Figure 4

Thing Two

The issue of tension in stranded color knitting is both simple and exigent. The key is to carry the unworked strand across the back of the working stitches loosely enough that it doesn't pull in the work and cause puckers, and at the same time, tightly enough that it doesn't create loose stitches at the color-change boundaries. For example, let's say you want to work five stitches with color A, five with color B, then five more with color A. To begin, knit the five A stitches, leaving the B strand hanging where it was last used **(Figure 1)**. Drop strand A and pick up strand B from *underneath* strand A, then stretch the five A stitches just worked as far apart on the right needle as you can comfortably get them **(Figure 2)**. Knit the next five stitches with strand B (carrying it straight across the back of first five A stitches), then drop strand B **(Figure 3)**. Pick up strand A from *over* the top of strand B, stretching the five B stitches as before **(Figure 4)**, then knit the next five stitches with strand A. Continue in this manner, always picking up A (the receding color) *over* B and always picking up B (the dominant color) *under* A. Trust me, this is much easier than it sounds.

Figure 1

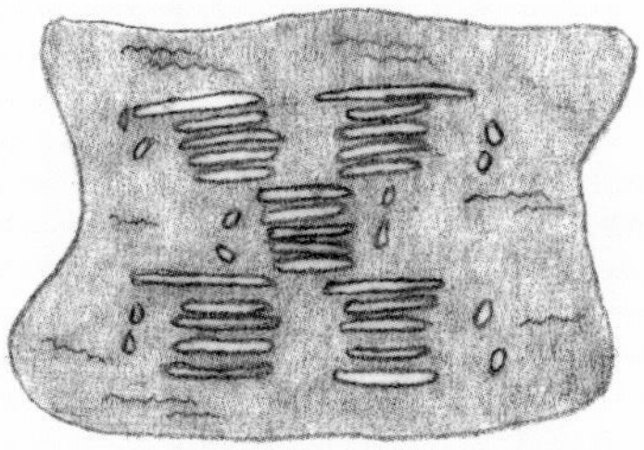
Figure 2

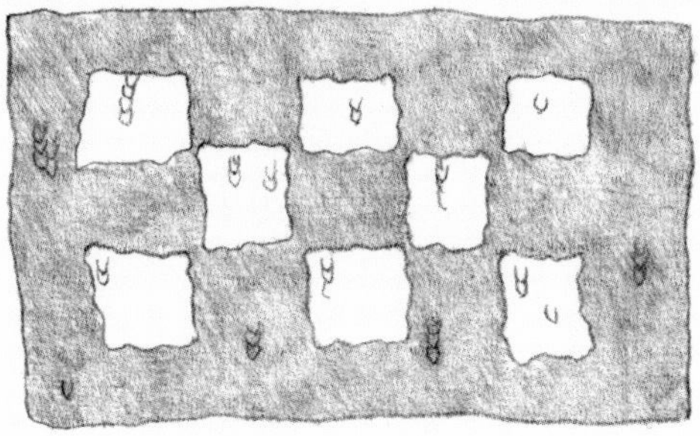
Figure 3

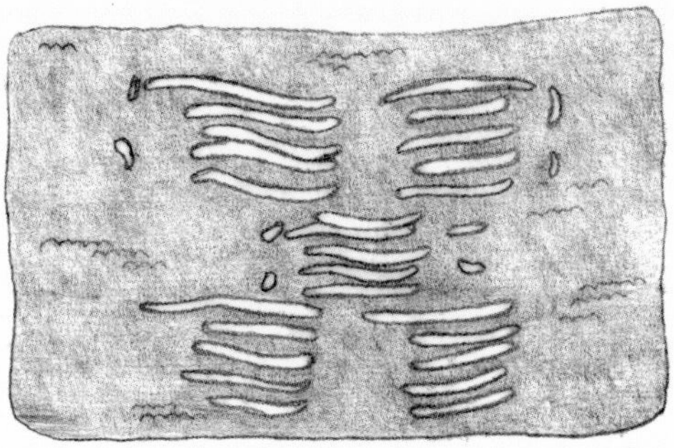
Figure 4

If your tension is correct, the stitches will all be the same size, and the floats of A and B will form parallel horizontal paths across the back of the work. If your tension is too tight, the fabric will draw together and lack elasticity **(Figures 1 and 2)**. If your tension is too loose, some of the stitches will be looser (larger) than others and the strands will hang in loose loops across the back **(Figures 3 and 4)**. Fortunately, both of these problems are easily avoided if you pay attention as you knit. Be patient as you get the feel for the tension you like best, and don't be surprised if your opinions of what is right change as you gain experience.

Tacky, Tacky

In stranded color knitting, the unused strands of yarn "float" across the non-public (wrong) side of the work. Long floats that span ten or more stitches (or several inches) should be secured to the back of the knitting so they won't get caught on things (fingernails, fence posts, etc.) when the garment is worn. The act of anchoring a float is called "tacking."

Whether or not to tack floats, and when to do so, is probably as old and controversial a topic as the chicken and the egg. For every knitter who says to always tack floats, you'll likely find one who says to never tack. Ultimately, the decision is yours. If you haven't already developed your own preferences, try it my way until you feel comfortable.

To tack a float, simply twist the floating strand around the working strand after every four to eight stitches. How often to tack is subjective: a ten-stitch float may need to be tacked just once but a fourteen-stitch float might be tacked twice. Tacking the floats will complicate your knitting, for which you need to compensate.

Complication #1: The color of the tacked float will always, no matter what, show a little bit between stitches on the public side of the work.

To counteract this,

- Tack floats as infrequently as possible.
- When tacking floats for several successive rows, stagger the tacking points as much as possible to diminish their appearance on the front—don't tack floats in the same place on successive rows.

Complication #2: The two strands of yarn become more tangled with every tack.

To minimize (but not eliminate) this,

- Tack floats as infrequently as possible.
- Hold one strand of yarn in your right hand (and work it following the English method of knitting) and hold the other strand of yarn in your left hand (and work it following the Continental method of knitting) so that you are between the two balls of yarn. **Note:** It is not necessary to know how to knit in the Continental style to make stranded colorwork; this myth probably stems from the fact that Fair Isle knitters frequently are also Continental knitters (who happen to tack their floats like crazy. Hmm . . .).
- Alternate the direction in which the strands are twisted for each tack.

Complication #3: Tacks compromise the overall tension of the work if the float is carried too loosely or too tightly between uses, or if tacks result in accidental reversals between the dominant and receding strands (see page 115). In extreme cases, the tacks can affect the orientation and appearance of the stitches on the front of the work.

To prevent this,

- Tack floats as infrequently as possible.
- Pay careful attention to the tension of the floats that do require tacking.
- Remember to return both strands to their original positions (top and bottom) after every tack.

By now, you can surmise that I am neither a frequent nor willing tacker of floats. My advice is to pay close attention to the front of the work. If at any point the stitches don't look right on the front, take a look at what's happening on the back. Tacking floats is a necessary evil, to be sure, but not one that should undermine your fun.

HEMS

Many of my designs begin with folded hems. This is partly due to tradition and partly due to the fact that I don't like to knit ribbing. Hemmed edges have a tactical construction advantage, too. Although my instructions do not mention securing your hem until the finishing stage, you may find that securing it early makes the rest of the knitting easier. Once in place, hems add a little weight and stability to the lower edge of the work, which helps ensure even tension.

Casting On

A folded hem begins with casting on the desired number of stitches. With a bit of cleverness, you can cast on in a way that will help you later. I like to cast on with a circular needle at least two sizes larger than the size I plan to use for the body of the knitting so that the cast-on stitches are a bit loose. If the main body will be worked on a size 3 (3.25 mm) needle, for example, I look under the sofa until I locate a size 5 (3.75 mm). Then I round up a bunch of stitch markers. These are optional, but I'm a lousy counter, and they help me keep track during the inevitable interruptions. I use the knitted method (see Glossary) to cast on, which is not to be confused with the cable method, its useful, but bulkier, cousin. I cast on the required number of stitches, placing a marker every 50 or 100 stitches to help me keep count along the way.

If the sweater is a cardigan, I don't join the round (yet). Instead, I work flat for the length of the hem because joining and beginning the steek at this point adds unnecessary bulk, and working flat makes it easier to ensure that the stitches don't get twisted when I do join them for working in rounds. If the sweater is a pullover, there's no choice but to make the join.

Use Silamide, a wax-permeated thread available at beading supply shops, for the invisible handsewing on facings and trims. It buries itself beautifully in the work and will not knot or kink as you work.

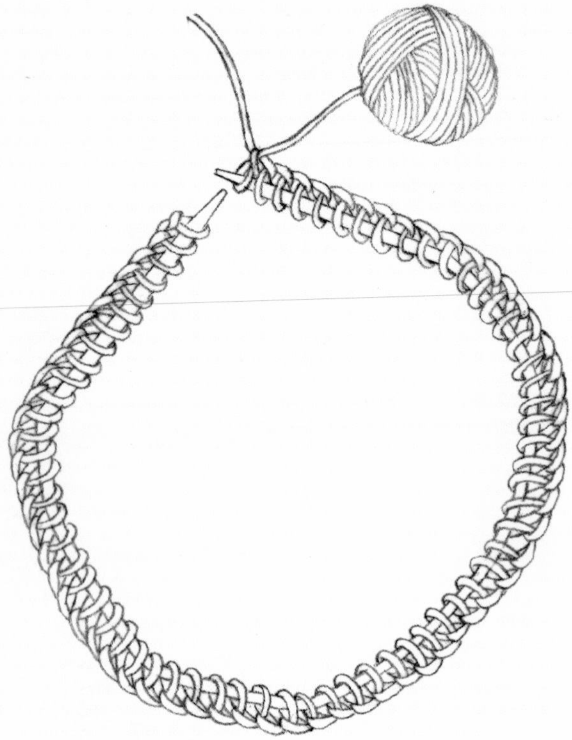

Before joining, make sure that all of the loops are on top of the needle and all of the "knots" are on the bottom.

When you see a circular needle with three hundred stitches on it, you will understand why the words "being careful not to twist the stitches" are always in circular knitting instructions. If the stitches are twisted around the cable of the circular needle when you start working in rounds, your knitting will be twisted and instead of forming a straight tube, you'll form a twisted mess. My first stranded colorwork sweater was twisted on the needles and had to be ripped out by my mother (I was busy sobbing) after four inches of work. Prevent this by making sure the loops are all on the top of the needle and the "knots" are all on the bottom, as shown at left.

Facing

The first few rows of knitting will become the facing for the hem. To reduce bulk, work the facing with a needle that is one or two sizes smaller than the one you'll use for the main body. If the main body will be worked on a size 3 (3.25 mm) needle, for example, use a size 1 (2.25 mm) for the facing. Work the facing in stockinette stitch for the same depth as the desired hem.

Turning Edge

Now the excitement begins. The turning edge is a row (or round) of knitting that forms a natural fold line. It is either a ridge of purl stitches worked on a right-side row or a picot ridge that alternates knitting two stitches together (k2tog) with a yarnover (yo). When working a purl ridge, I like to use the same small needle (or even a smaller one, depending on the yarn and my whim) that I used for the facing for a firm tidy ridge. When working a picot ridge, I like to use the larger needle I will use for the main body to produce nicely pronounced points.

You are now ready to begin on the public side of the work. If you haven't already, switch to the needle you will be using for the main knitting. Work the prescribed number of rows for this half of the hem, which is usually the same number as you worked for the facing.

Secure the Facing

There are two ways to secure the facing to the sweater body. You can continue to knit the body for a few inches and sew the facing in place or you can knit the facing in place on the first row of the body.

Sewn-In Method

After knitting the body for at least a few inches (enough to hold onto), fold the facing along the turning edge and use a sewing needle and matching thread to sew the cast-on edge to the wrong side. This is a fail-safe method for producing an invisible hem. If you don't mind the curling edge of the facing, you can postpone this step until you've finished knitting the body. My experience is that securing the hem as early in the process as I can makes knitting the body easier.

Knitted-In Method

Because of your cleverness during the cast on, your first row of knitting is loose enough to knit in the hem by working the cast-on stitches together with the corresponding live stitches on the next row of the body. You'll use the larger needle you used to cast-on with (a size 5 [3.75 mm] needle in our example) for this row. Fold the facing to the wrong side along the turning edge, insert the larger needle through the first live stitch of the body as if to knit, then through the first loop of the cast-on row, and then knit them together as if they were a single stitch. Do the same for every stitch on the needle. The first few stitches will be awkward, but be patient and persevere. After a few stitches, check the public side of the work to ensure that the hem is straight and that the live stitches are correctly aligned with the cast-on loops. The hem will appear slanted if the stitches are not properly aligned. If this happens, you'll need to rip out and begin again—otherwise the slanting will only get worse. At the end of the round, the hem will be secured invisibly in place. Change back to the body needle and work the rest of the body as indicated in the instructions.

Tack floats to the back of a stitch that is the same color so they will be less visible on the right side of the knitting.

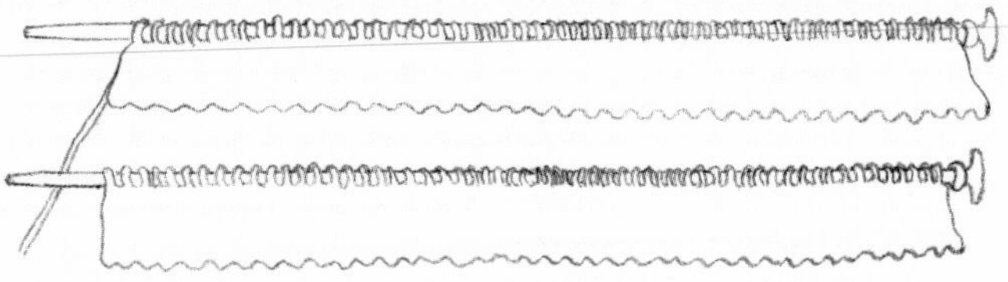

Figure 1

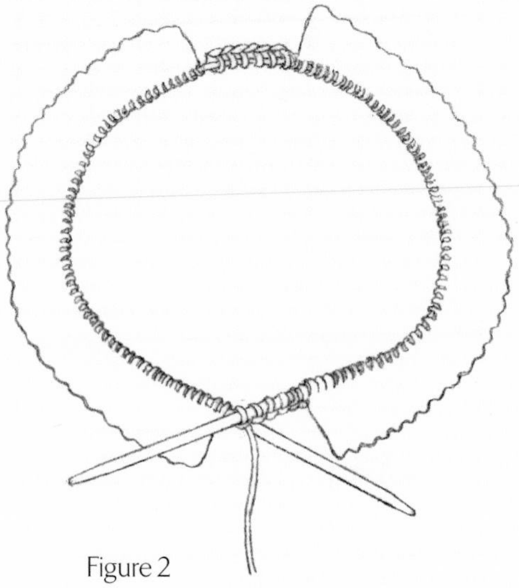

Figure 2

SLEEVES

With the exception of Wedding Belle (page 92), all of the sleeves featured in this book are worked circularly, beginning with a wrist-size cuff, shaped with increases centered along the inside "seam," and ending with a few rows of reverse stockinette stitch that form a facing to cover the armhole cut edge. Because the garments have drop-shoulder shaping, there are no sleeve caps to shape—the stitches are bound off when the sleeve is the desired length.

In some projects, I chose to work both sleeves at the same time. Infant- and child-size sleeves are often easier (and faster) to knit two at a time. I move a lot faster using a 16" (40 cm) circular needle than working with five double-pointed needles, but your mileage may vary. I also prefer to knit sleeves simultaneously if the pattern involves a trillion color changes along the length of the sleeve. I'd rather cut the sleeves apart and sew seams (that I cover with bias tape on the wrong side) than weave in all those yarn tails.

To work two sleeves simultaneously, begin by working the two cuffs or hems flat **(Figure 1)**. With a circular needle, work across the stitches of one cuff, cast on extra stitches for a steek, work across the stitches of the other cuff, cast on extra stitches for another steek, then join for working in rounds **(Figure 2)**. Work the shaping increases adjacent to each set of steek stitches as instructed in the pattern directions. When the sleeves are the desired length, bind off just the steek stitches, place the sleeve stitches on waste yarn holders **(Figure 3)**, then machine stitch to secure the knitting **(Figure 4)** and cut the two pieces apart. Seam the cut edges, then work the facing from the live stitches. You can cover the raw edges of the sleeve seam with ribbon or bias tape.

Increases

The sleeves widen from the cuff circumference to the upper arm circumference by increases worked at regular intervals, just like sleeves worked flat. Unlike in flat knitting, however, these

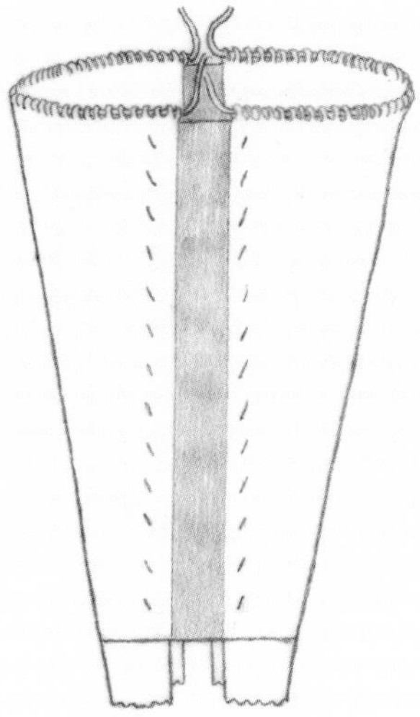

Figure 3

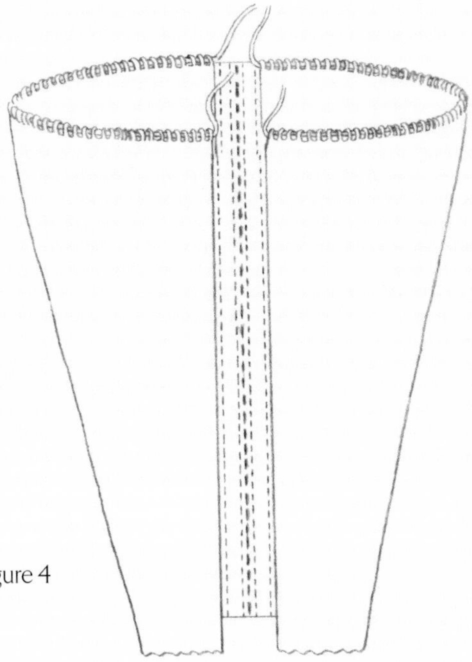

Figure 4

increases are made in the very first and in the very last stitch of each round, rather than two or three stitches in from the edge, to minimize interruptions in the charted pattern. I typically use bar increases (knit into the front and back of the same stitch; see Glossary) because they are unobtrusive and do not create holes in the knitting. But feel free to use the increase method of your choice.

The increases are typically worked every five or six rows from the top of the cuff to the top of the sleeve. For a drop-shoulder sleeve, the total length is more important than the exact number of stitches at the top of the sleeve. For this reason, the number of stitches at the top (and the corresponding width measurement) will vary according to the sleeve length. You will cut a slit in the body to match the width of the upper sleeve. In other words, you will make the armhole fit your sleeve top, rather than the other way around. This notion is the exact opposite from flat-knitted sleeves and armholes. Relax and roll with it—you'll appreciate the simplicity once you work with it. This cavalier approach also gives you complete license to adjust the length without performing any other calculations.

Facing

To finish the sleeve, knit a facing that will cover the cut edges of the armhole steek. This is a simple matter of knitting a few rounds (typically six) in reverse stockinette stitch. If you don't like to purl (or have forgotten how after knitting in the round all that time), just turn your work around and knit from the wrong side. This will make a very tiny hole at the turning point, but it will be on the inside of the sweater where no one will see it. When working the facing, increase one stitch at each end (in the first and last stitch) of every round to form a little gusset that will ensure a good fit over and around the cut armhole edges. When the facing is the desired length, bind off all the stitches. It's important that the bind-off be worked loosely—I usually use a needle two or three sizes larger than I used to knit the sleeve.

STEEKS ARE OUR FRIENDS

The mere mention of the word "steek" is enough to send some tightly wound knitters straight to the nearest Stitchers Anonymous meeting. And it's no wonder. The ambiguity surrounding the concept is nearly mythic. Even the word itself is no help—it's both a noun ("the steek") and a verb ("to steek"), for Pete's sake. Designers and teachers don't help much either, casually throwing steeks into patterns with no real instruction, the way they do. But before you go fetal, give me a chance to demystify the concept. As with everything else in knitting, steeks are no big deal if you approach them with equally sharp wits and scissors. If, after we're through, you still want to run away leaving a knitter-shaped hole in the wall, do so with my blessing.

First, let's clear up the semantics. Yes, the steek is a noun, which refers to an area of waste (like a seam allowance) where the knitting will be cut after due preparation. There are different kinds of steeks to be found in *The New Stranded Colorwork*—along the center front of the body (for cardigans), along the sides of the body (for armholes), at the top of the body (for front neck shaping), and between two sleeves that are worked simultaneously. *To steek* is a verb, which means to secure the waste area with machine stitches and then to cut it open. So you could actually say that you are steeking a steek, as in "Not now darling, Mommy's steeking a steek. Ask Daddy to put out the fire, please."

Beginning the Steek

Some steeks are just areas where you will slash into perfectly normal knitting with your shears. Others are places where you cast on some extra stitches that you know will be sacrificed later. All of the projects in this book use six-stitch steeks, which is what I'll describe here. You may encounter (and prefer) narrower or wider steeks as you gain experience.

Place a marker at the beginning of the steek stitches. Next, cast on six new stitches, using the backward-loop (fast and dirty), knitted (slower but more stable), or cable (slowest and most reliable) method (see Glossary for all methods), alternating one stitch each of each color, if there are two colors in that round of knitting. Place another marker after the last steek stitch and continue working in rounds, being careful not to twist the steek stitches (see page 120). Continue working the body stitches in the charted pattern and alternate the colors across the six steek stitches every round. Alternating colors in the steek stitches in the same order every round produces vertical stripes that will come in handy when it's time to stitch and cut the steek, or you can alternate them in a birds-eye pattern for a very stable steek. Work the steek stitches in stockinette stitch.

Ending the Steek

Ending a steek is even easier than beginning one. Only armhole steeks need to be bound off because the top edges are subject to a lot of stress; steeks worked along the center front or neck will be stitched and cut separately, which I'll discuss later. To begin, locate the steek stitches (either by counting or by looking between two stitch markers) and bind them off with a crochet hook as follows: Working from the center of the steek to the left, chain the fourth steek stitch over the fifth, then chain the fifth stitch over the sixth, then chain the sixth over the adjoining body stitch **(Figure 1)**. Turn the work around

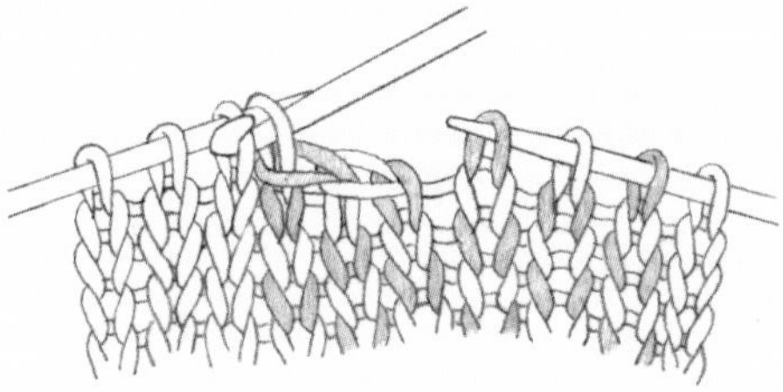

Figure 1

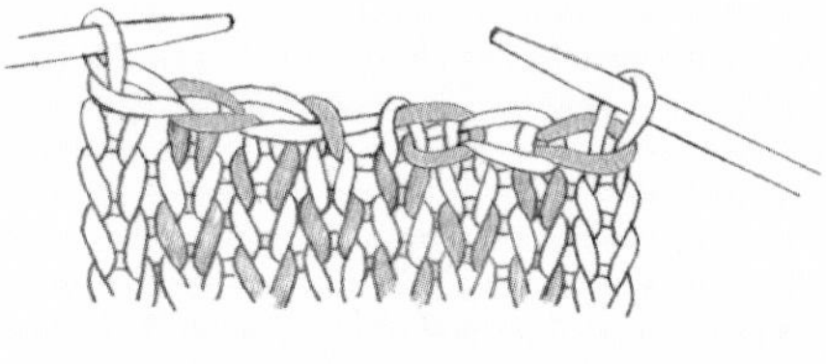

Figure 2

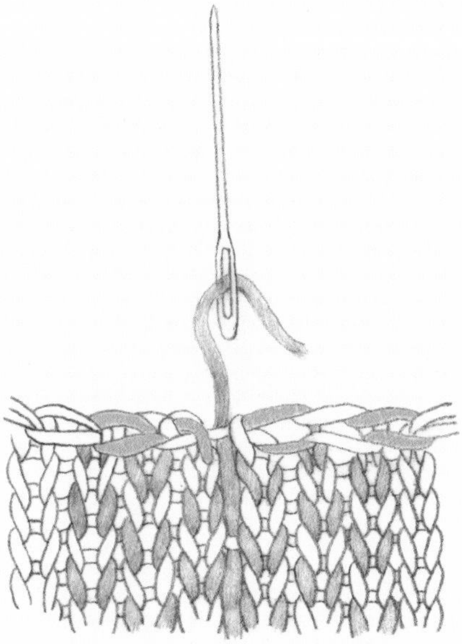

Figure 1

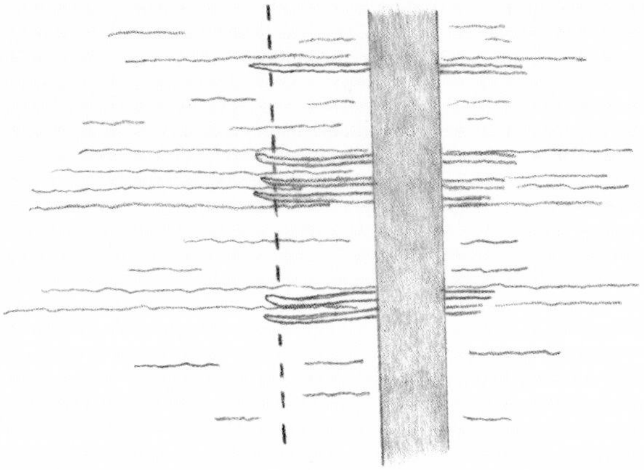

Figure 2

so the wrong side is facing you and working from right to left, chain the third steek stitch over the second, then chain the second over the first, then chain the first over the adjoining body stitch. When viewed from the right side, the first three steek stitches will angle to the right and the second three steek stitches will angle to the left **(Figure 2)**. That's all there is to it. Your armhole steek has now come to an end.

Marking

To mark a steek, find one of those shiny new tapestry needles you cleverly stocked up on and thread it with highly contrasting yarn. The brighter the yarn, the better you will be able to see it, so don't hold back the really ghastly stuff from the neighbor's yard sale; this is its true calling. Use this yarn to baste a vertical line of stitches up the very center of the steek, between the third and fourth stitches **(Figure 1)**. Be sure not to pull this marking yarn so tight that it disappears in the knitting—the whole point is to be able to see it clearly. Next, thread your well-oiled sewing machine with an equally contrasting thread; again, uglier really is better. Don't forget to change the machine needle to a nice sharp one, too—you deserve every possible advantage you can get. Turn on all the lights in the room and put on your glasses.

Before you continue, here's a bit of trickery you can perform to amaze your friends, or at least the cat, if he's watching. Turn your sweater inside out. The dozens of yarn tails adjoining the steek will resemble the floor of the Muppet's barber shop. What a mess! You trusted me and tied all those little knots and now look at the hairy hoard of yarn ends hiding inside your beautiful sweater! Take a deep breath and locate your trusty painters' tape (look under the chair where your children last restrained the babysitter/grandparent/health inspector; that's where mine always ends up). Next, lay your sweater on something flat and use your fingers to gently untangle and comb all the yarn tails horizontally across the center of the steek. Tape the yarn tails a couple of inches away from the steek **(Figure 2)** to prevent them from interfering with the machine stitching. That's it. Turn the work right side out again and you're ready to move along.

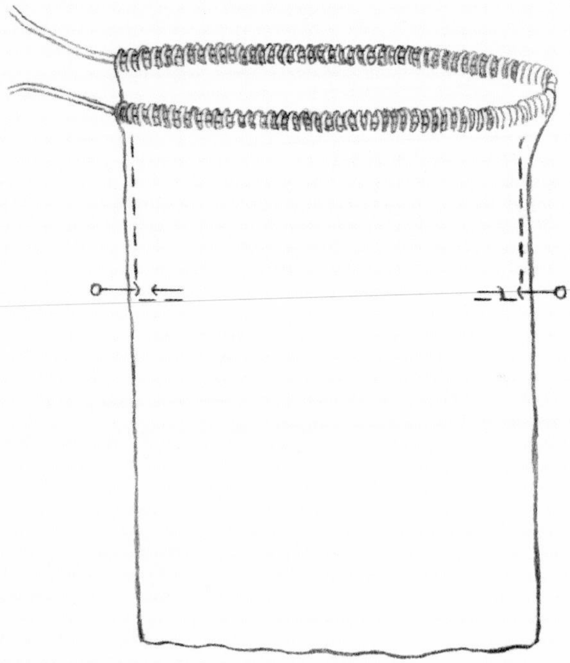

For an armhole opening, you won't know exactly how far to cut until you've measured the width (one-half of the circumference) at the top of the sleeve. For best results, measure the width of each sleeve and take the average. Measure this length down from the shoulder line on each side of the body for the armhole depth. With contrasting yarn, baste a vertical line of marking stitches, then mark a short horizontal line of stitches at the desired armhole depth as shown above.

Machine Stitching

Wrestle the sweater under the presser foot of your sewing machine (threaded with a highly contrasting color). With the machine set for a medium-size straight stitch, sew a straight line from the top of the steek to the bottom to the left of the marking yarn, right through the middle of the vertical line made by the fourth knitted steek stitch **(Figure 1)**. Sew another straight line to the right of the marking yarn, right through the middle of the vertical line made by the third knitted steek stitch **(Figure 2)**. Make a third pass through the middle of the vertical line made by the sixth knitted steek stitch, then a fourth pass through the middle of the vertical line made by the first knitted steek stitch. You now have four vertical lines of machine stitching, which are more or less straight if you turned on all the lights **(Figure 3)**. All that's left is to cut open the steek, which is hopefully less intimidating now that you've secured the knitting with machine stitching.

Cutting

To save wear and tear on your last nerve while you cut your knitting, get a piece of cardboard, glossy magazine, kitchen cutting board, or other portable smooth surface. I like to use the laminated copy of the charts that I've been dragging around in my knitting bag—it seems like poetic justice to me. Stick the smooth thing inside your sweater. Presto! Your razor-sharp shears are no longer in danger of accidentally catching a float on the back of the garment that you are hoping not to eviscerate. Now quit playing around and cut the thing, already. Knitting is not for wimps, and if you have gotten this far only to chicken out, I'll come to your house to taunt you in person. Slice the steek with authority and surgical precision, right down the middle of your ugly-yarn marking stitches. All that remains is to pull out the remaining bits of marking yarn.

There. You did it. You steeked the steek. It's time for the final step, as soon as the trembling stops. I'm sorry I got rough with you back there, but a person who is holding the shears over a year's worth of knitting needs a firm hand, not molly-coddling. It's no time to flinch, and I knew you could take it. The optional final step is to retreat to your happy place (bathtub? manicurist? yarn shop?) and recite your tale of glory for all to hear. If you're not up to gloating yet, at least enjoy the beverage of your choice, and congratulate yourself on a job well done.

Once you've hacked open a sweater, you can do anything. Well done, Grasshopper.

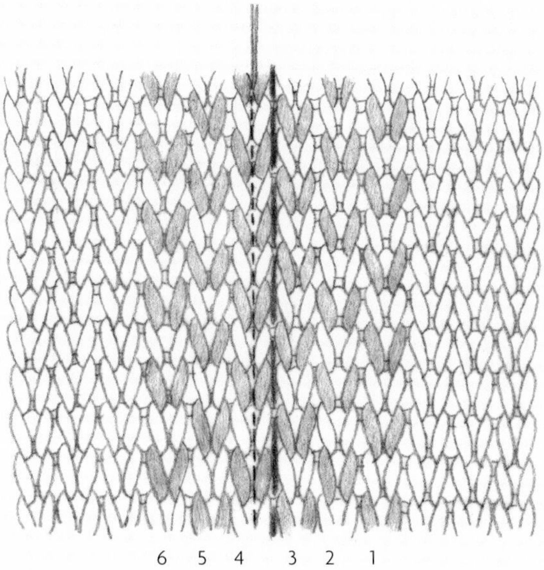

Figure 1

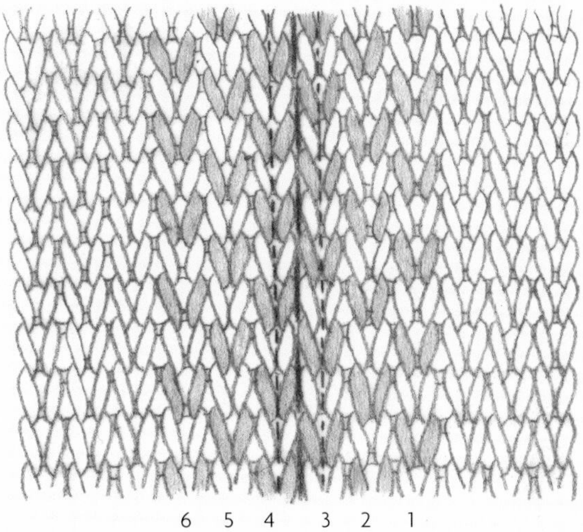

Figure 2

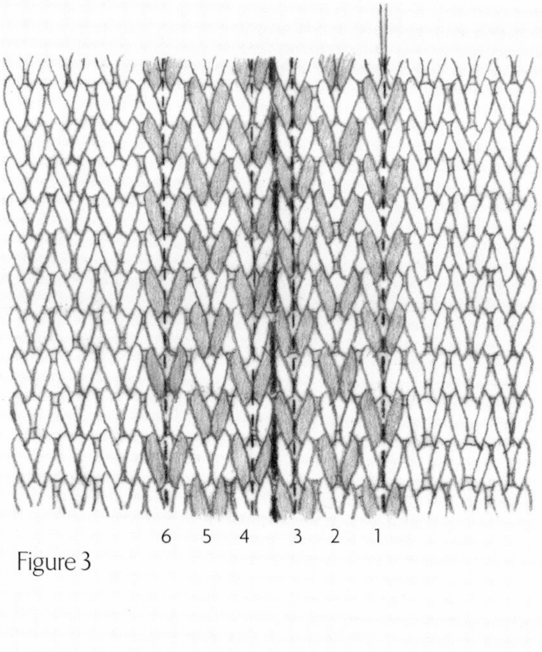

Figure 3

A trick for choosing colors: Start with a few shades you know you like together, then ask yourself "What is the color I am least likely to add?" Now include that color in the group. The results may surprise you.

FINISHING

It is difficult to find information specific to the finishing of stranded color knitting and I believe that's because much knitting never does get finished. I won't sugar-coat it: It takes time to finish knitwear that has been shaped by steeks. If you decided to knit in the round because you wanted to avoid finishing, this phase of construction may disappoint you. Although it's true that there are fewer seams to sew, there are also more edges to conceal. I often find that it takes as long (or longer) to finish a sweater as it takes to knit it, but I tend to lengthen the process because I enjoy it so much. I am, by nature, a person who likes fiddly handwork. The prospect of sewing on seven different ribbon trims by hand is one that I meet with glee and then I often ask if some sequins might be called for, too. Too much trimming is never enough in my estimation. If you are not similarly inclined, then blessings are on you. You will finish and enjoy your sweater all the sooner, and you will never have to explain why you wear a sweater with fifty pounds of crystal beads to the grocery store.

There are really only a few steps necessary to beautifully complete a piece of stranded color knitting—blocking, neckline shaping, seaming, covering edges, and trims and closures. Skip any at your whim or peril. But try to keep an open mind—you may find that you enjoy the process as much as the finished product.

Blocking

Blocking is the gentle art of getting your yarn to lie flat and behave once it is in fabric form. This is fun and easy to do in the case of tubular construction because nearly all of the edges are nice and straight. Block body pieces before cutting the neck and armhole steeks, using the method called for by the yarn you used (check the ball band). Be as gentle or assertive as needed, but do get the job done. Lay the piece flat in a place where it won't be disturbed until it is completely dry. I have used the guestroom bed, the spare bathroom floor, and the top of the refrigerator with varying degrees of success.

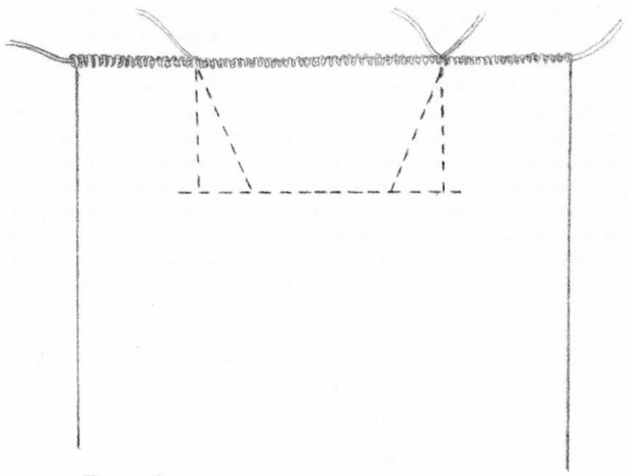

Figure 1

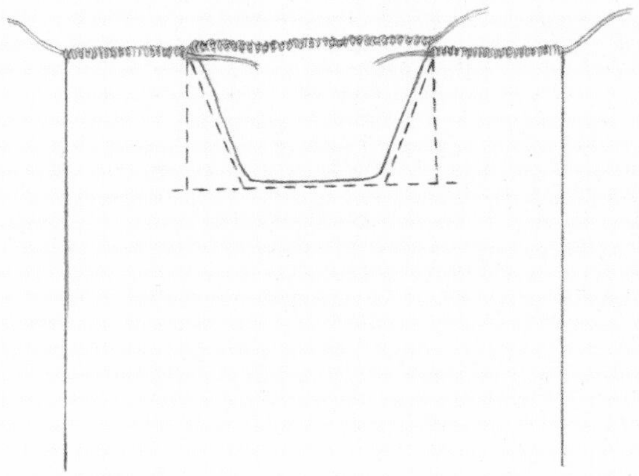

Figure 2

Neckline Shaping

In stranded colorwork knitting, holes for heads are made by cutting into the tube of knitted fabric, rather than shaping flat pieces that are seamed together. Aside from overcoming the trepidation that accompanies cutting holes in your knitting, there are only two things to know about shaping necklines—how wide and how deep to cut them. The position of the neck hole is evident once you have divided the stitches in the finished body tube as directed. The instructions will specify a particular depth, but feel free to make your own adjustments wherever you wish.

Marking

Use contrasting waste yarn threaded on a tapestry needle to mark the neck opening. To begin, mark a vertical line at each side of the desired neck width from the top edge of the body to the desired depth. These lines mark the width of the neckline. Next, mark a horizontal line at the desired neck depth, connecting the two vertical lines. If you want a square neckline, skip to the stitching and cutting directions below. To produce a curved neckline, mark a 45-degree slope between the vertical and horizontal lines **(Figure 1)**. You can adjust these sloped lines to your liking.

Machine Stitching

With contrasting thread, machine stitch along the marking lines, then stitch a second line about ½" (1.3 cm) next to (inside) the first stitches. Remove the basting yarn.

Cutting

Now use your sharp shears to cut the knitted fabric close to the second line of machine stitches **(Figure 2)**. That's all there is to it! The raw edges will be covered later with knitted binding. Please do yourself the kindness of having sharp shears, good lighting, and a calm disposition available for this operation. Don't think too hard about it; just remove everything that isn't neck hole.

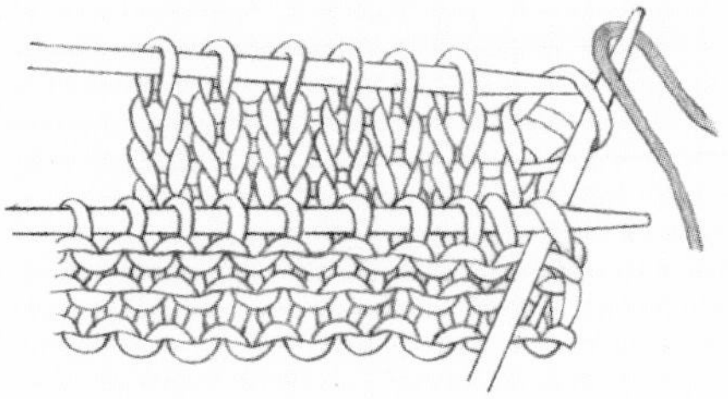
Figure 1

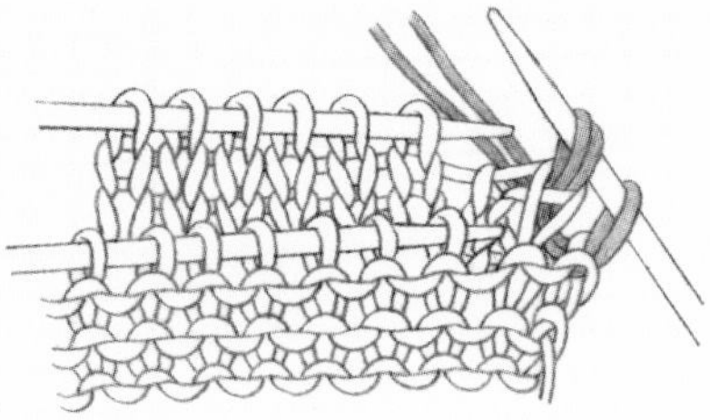
Figure 2

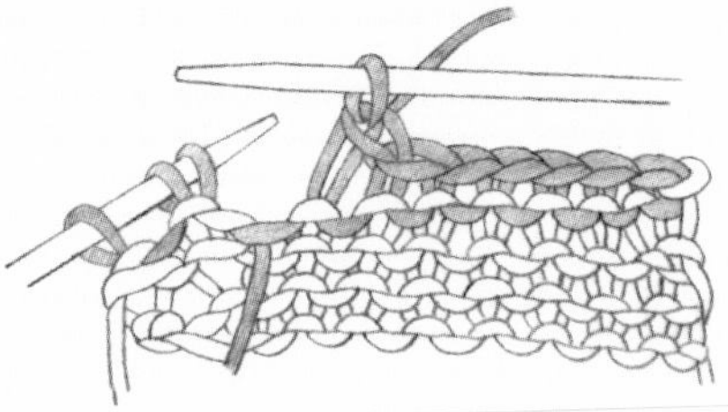
Figure 3

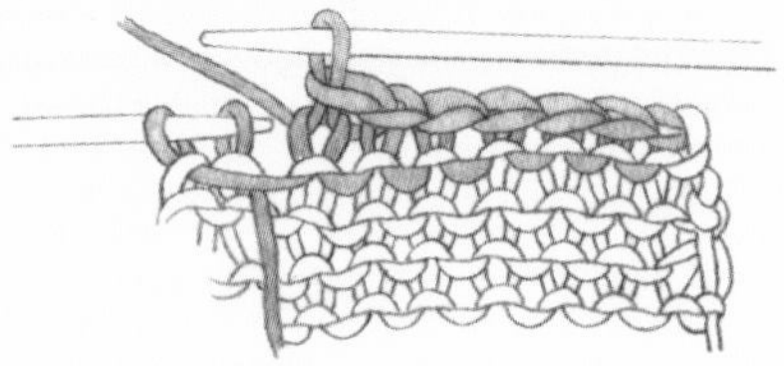
Figure 4

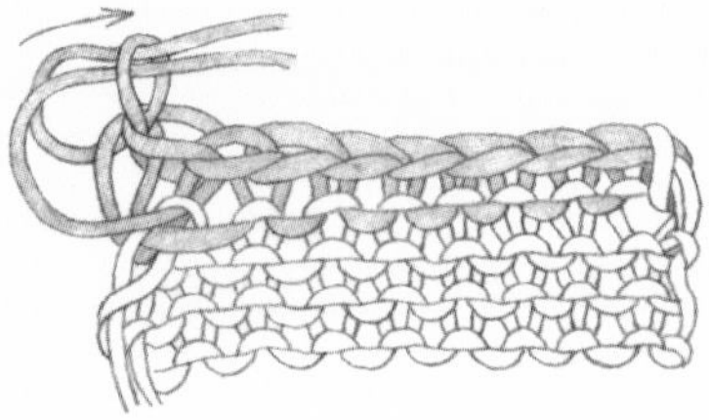
Figure 5

Shoulder Seams

The shoulder seams in all of the projects in this book are joined with a three-needle bind-off. In my opinion, this makes the least bulky and most secure shoulder seam. Not all three-needle bind-offs are created equal; the two-row version I use easily supports the weight of the entire sweater, which is its purpose, after all. (The more conventional method is provided in the Glossary.)

You will need three needles of the same size used to knit the sweater body. The needles can be straight, double-pointed, circular, or a combination thereof. Place the front shoulder stitches on one needle and the corresponding back shoulder stitches on a second so that the armhole edge stitches are at the needle points. Hold the needles parallel with the right sides of the knitting facing together (you'll be looking at the wrong side of the garment) and with both points facing to the right. You will bind off from the armhole edge to the neck edge.

Row 1: With yarn that matches the color of the stitches being joined and leaving a tail about 6" (15 cm) long, insert the third needle into the first stitch on each needle and knit them together **(Figure 1)**. Hold the tail and working yarn together and knit the next stitch on each needle together—this stitch will consist of two loops of yarn **(Figure 2)**. Drop the tail and continue to knit all of the stitches from the first two needles together—all of the stitches will be on the third needle. Turn the work around.

Row 2: Slip the first stitch knitwise, *knit the next stitch, then pass the first stitch over the second stitch and off the needle. Repeat from * until you reach the second-to-last (doubled) stitch **(Figure 3)**. Drop one of the two strands off the needle and pull on the original tail to eliminate the slack **(Figure 4)**. Bind off the remaining two stitches. Break the working yarn, thread both tails through the remaining stitch **(Figure 5)**, and pull tight to secure.

Tie the two strands together in an overhand knot for extra security, if desired, then trim the tails to about 1" (2.5 cm) long. The tails will be hidden under the facing.

Picking Up Stitches

It has been my observation that the number of knitters who think they know how to pick up and knit stitches (or "knit up stitches" as our friends in the United Kingdom say) does not always equate to the number who really know how. Whichever camp you fall into, it's a good idea to take a quick review.

Machine stitching and cutting creates a number of unsightly raw edges that need to be covered both for aesthetics and durability. This is done with knitted-on edgings, often referred to as bindings. Bindings are just like hemmed edges except that rather than beginning with live stitches, we have to pick up the first row of stitches.

There are two aspects to picking up stitches—picking them up in the right place and picking up the right number of them. Where to pick up stitches is usually established by the line of machine stitching adjoining the steek. Your goal should be to get the line of picked -p stitches as close to the machine stitches as possible, while covering them up with knitting. Whenever possible, pick up from the center of the existing stitches as shown here.

Figuring out how many stitches to pick up is less straightforward. It has been the subject of clever writings, most of which contain mathematical formulas that make my eyes glaze over. I'm told these formulas are extremely reliable and very useful, and those of you with the intellectual fortitude to grasp them have my deep and abiding respect. If you are like me, however, and not given to lasting relationships with numbers, do what I do—fake it. The number of stitches that pattern instructions specify to pick up is really just a guideline. No one is going to back you into a corner and count the stitches in your neckline facing, and if they do, you're attending the wrong parties. Trial and error are your friends in this pursuit, so trust them both, and write down what you learn to help you remember. When picking up stitches along a horizontal edge (such as the straight part of a neckline), pick up in every stitch. When picking up stitches along a vertical or mostly vertical edge (such as the curve of a neckline or a cardigan opening), pick up three stitches for every four rows of knitted fabric. After working a few rows of the edging, evaluate how it looks. If the edge appears to pucker or pull in too much, you've picked up too few stitches—rip out and try again picking up four stitches for every five rows. If, on the other hand, the edge flares, you've picked up too many stitches—rip out and try again picking up two stitches for every three rows.

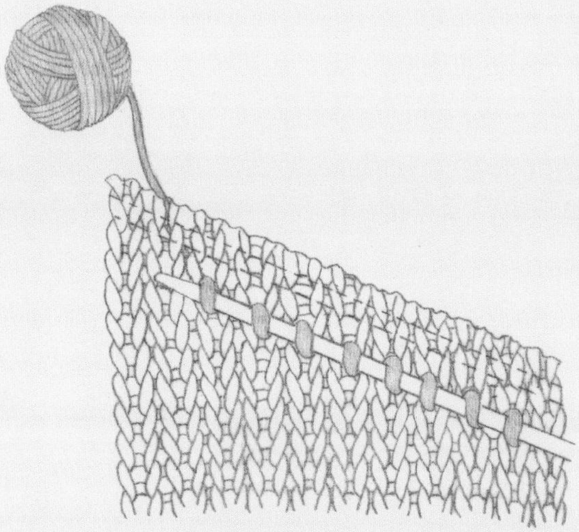

Armhole Seams

Advocates of circular knitting promise freedom from seams and they are right, as long as the sleeves are picked up and knitted from the armholes to the cuffs. However, all of the sleeves in this book are worked from the cuffs to the armholes and sewn in place. After the armhole openings are cut, use the three-needle method described above to join the shoulder stitches together. Place the body and sleeve on a table with the right sides facing outward. Using as many or as few pins as you like, join the sleeve to the armhole opening, making sure that the center of the sleeve aligns with the shoulder seam.

With yarn threaded on a tapestry needle, begin at the underarm and work your way around to the shoulder, then back down to the underarm, sewing the sleeve into the armhole. I typically leave an 8" (20.5 cm) length of seaming yarn unfastened at the underarm, rather than securing it, in case I don't like the way the seam looks and I decide to start over. For the drop-shoulder silhouettes used in this book, you will connect the tops of the stitches in the sleeve to the sides of the stitches along the armhole. Because stitches are slightly wider than they are long, there will not be a one-to-one ratio between the sleeve and body stitches. I usually have good results if I sew through every (horizontal) sleeve stitch, but only three out of every four (vertical) body stitches. There is a degree of trial and error in this process and it's not uncommon for me to adjust the ratio as I go or to ravel the seam and start again. When you are happy (or bored to death) with the seam, tie the two ends of the seaming yarn in an overhand knot. Pull them through to the wrong side, trim them to about 1" (2.5 cm) long, and fold the sleeve-top facing over the seam. Take a minute to marvel at the way the little gusset in the facing fits perfectly over the base of the armhole. Now you can see how like a plumbing flange it is, and how I came by that particular metaphor. I probably need to get out more.

Covering Raw Edges

After the sleeves are attached, some raw edges will need covering. Using the method described on page 131, pick up and knit stitches adjacent to the edges to make small (five- or six-row) facings. Use a needle two sizes larger to bind off the facing stitches to ensure that they are soft and flexible. Pin the facing over the raw edge, then lightly steam it. With a sharp hand-sewing needle and matching thread, sew the facing invisibly in place. If you prefer not to knit your facings, you can purchase an array of beautiful, flexible, stretchable, and folded bindings at a fabric store. I wholeheartedly support their use, particularly if it gets your sweater done quicker and prevents you from cursing me for leaving you with raw edges in the first place.

Trims and Closures

While you are at the fabric store, pick up any pretty closures, ribbons, or trims that strike your fancy. Your budget and your taste are the only limits here, so I encourage you to take advantage of the possibilities. Allow for the sweater to stretch a bit when pinning on ribbons and trims. Some puckering in the trims is both necessary and desirable in order for the sweater to move. Measure carefully between the closures to ensure that they are evenly spaced, then sew them in place securely with sewing thread. I often purchase an extra button or clasp and sew it to an unobtrusive spot inside the sweater (such as near the hem of the "side seam"). That I will lose one later is a mathematical certainty.

Please consider adding a label to your finished piece, as a finale. Use a permanent fabric marker to write the date, your name, and the name of the recipient on a piece of muslin sewn on the inside of the sweater. Years from now when you have forgotten all of the work and learning that went into this project, I'd like you and its wearer(s) to remember that its moment of completion was worthy of mark.

ABBREVIATIONS

beg(s)	begin(s); beginning
BO	bind off
CC	contrasting color
cm	centimeter(s)
cn	cable needle
CO	cast on
cont	continue(s); continuing
dec(s)	decrease(s); decreasing
dpn	double-pointed needles
foll	follow(s); following
g	gram(s)
inc(s)	increase(s); increasing
k	knit
k1f&b	knit into the front and back of same stitch
kwise	knitwise, as if to knit
m	marker(s)
MC	main color
mm	millimeter(s)
M1	make one (increase)
p	purl
p1f&b	purl into front and back of same stitch
patt(s)	pattern(s)
psso	pass slipped stitch over
pwise	purlwise, as if to purl
rem	remain(s); remaining
rep	repeat(s); repeating
rev St st	reverse stockinette stitch
rnd(s)	round(s)
RS	right side
sl	slip
sl st	slip st (slip 1 stitch purlwise unless otherwise indicated)
ssk	slip 2 stitches knitwise, one at a time, from the left needle to right needle, insert left needle tip through both front loops and knit together from this position (1 stitch decrease)
st(s)	stitch(es)
St st	stockinette stitch
tbl	through back loop
tog	together
WS	wrong side
wyb	with yarn in back
wyf	with yarn in front
yd	yard(s)
yo	yarnover
*	repeat starting point
* *	repeat all instructions between asterisks
( )	alternate measurements and/or instructions
[ ]	work instructions as a group a specified number of times

BIND-OFFS

Tubular 1 × 1 Rib Bind-Off

To set up for this bind-off, work two rows as foll: *K1, sl 1 pwise wyf; rep from *. Cut yarn, leaving an end three times as long as the width of the piece to be bound off.

Step 1: Insert tapestry needle from right to left through first knit stitch, pull yarn through, and slip this stitch off the needle **(Figure 1)**.

Step 2: Skip the next purl stitch, insert tapestry needle from right to left through the next knit stitch, pull the yarn through, and leave the stitch on the needle **(Figure 2)**.

Step 3: Insert tapestry needle from right to left through the skipped purl stitch, pull the yarn through, and slip both stitches off the needle **(Figure 3)**.

Step 4: Insert tapestry needle from left to right through the next purl stitch, pull the yarn through, and leave the stitch on the needle **(Figure 4)**.

Step 5: Insert tapestry needle from right to left through left half of previous knit stitch and pull the yarn through **(Figure 5)**.

Step 6: Insert tapestry needle from right to left in next knit stitch and pull the yarn through.

Repeat Steps 3–6 until all stitches have been bound off.

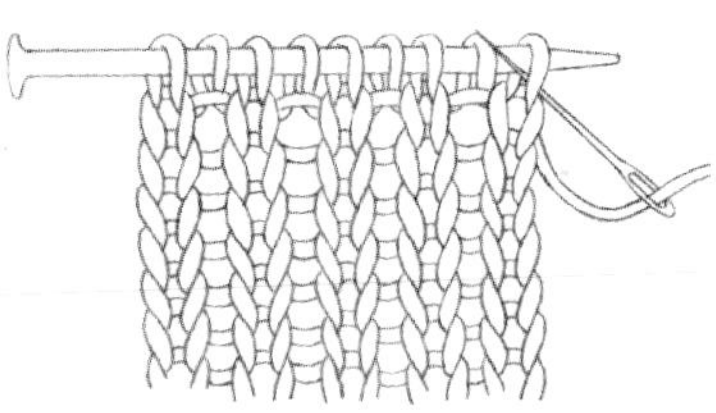

Figure 1

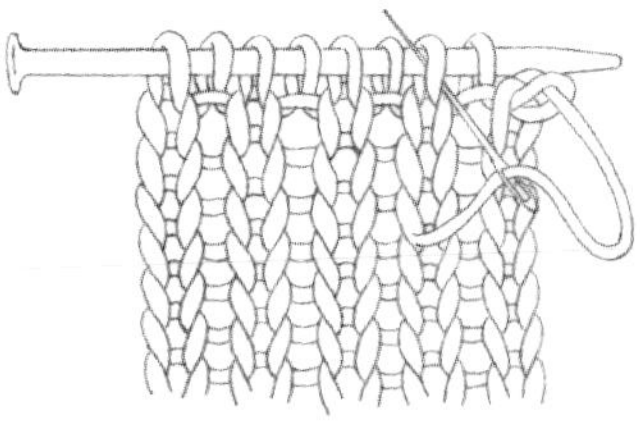

Figure 2

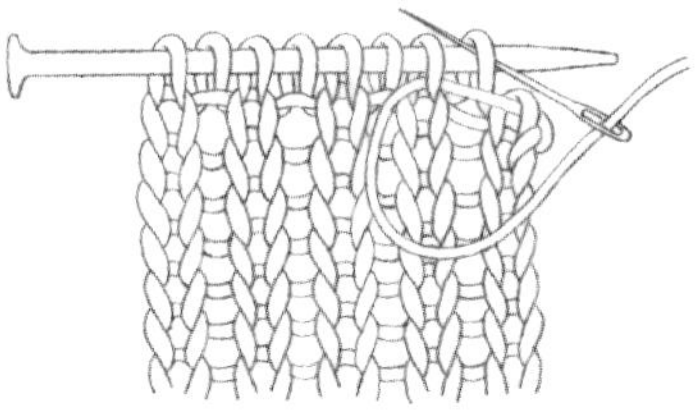

Figure 3

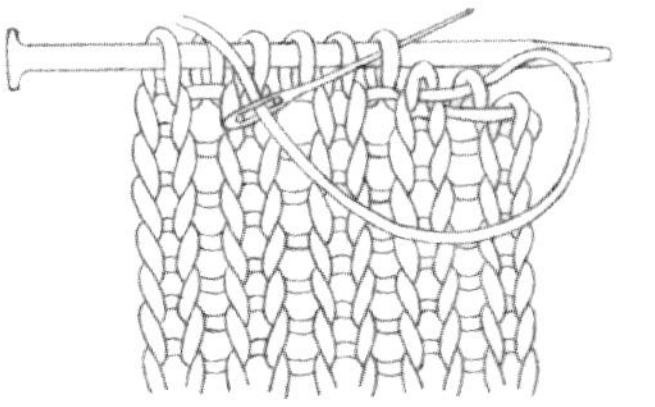

Figure 4

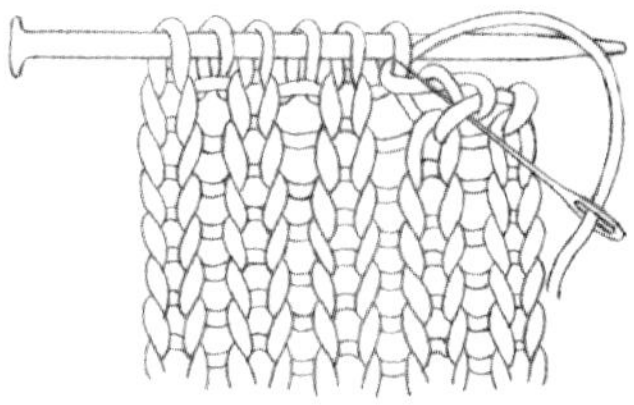

Figure 5

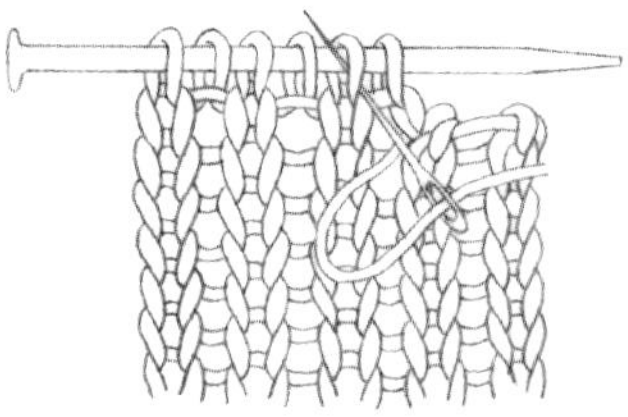

Figure 6

Standard Bind-Off

Knit the first stitch, *knit the next stitch (2 stitches on right needle), insert left needle tip into first stitch on right needle **(Figure 1)** and lift this stitch up and over the second stitch **(Figure 2)** and off the needle **(Figure 3)**. Repeat from * for the desired number of stitches.

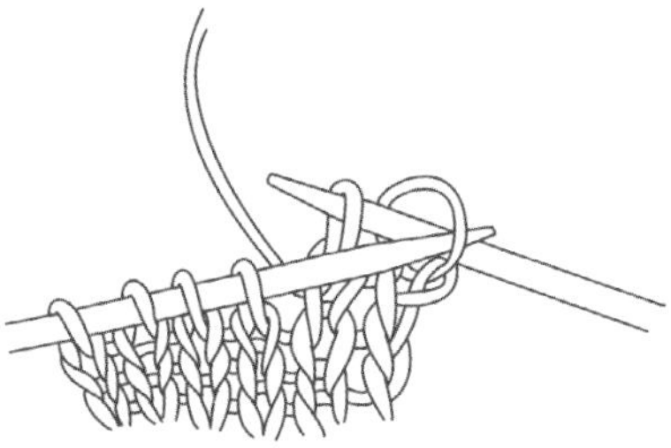

Figure 1

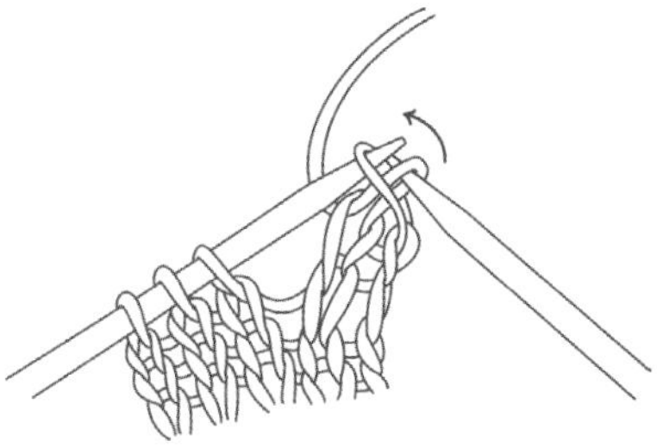

Figure 2

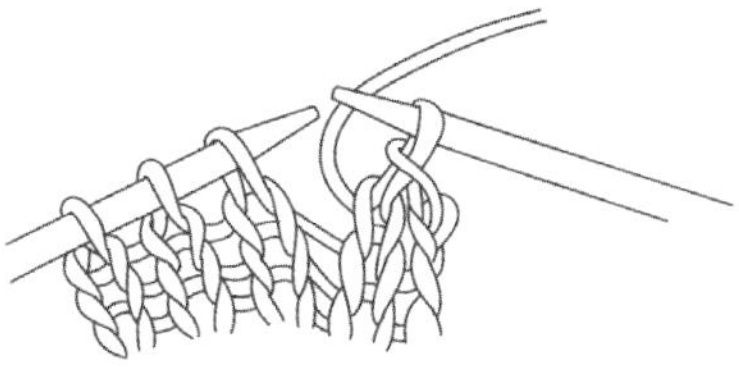

Figure 3

CAST-ONS

Backward-Loop Cast-On

*Loop working yarn and place it on needle backward so that it doesn't unwind. Repeat from *.

Cable Cast-On

If there are no stitches on the needles, make a slipknot of working yarn and place it on the needle, then use the knitted method at right to cast-on one more stitch—2 stitches on needle. Hold needle with working yarn in your left hand and *insert right needle between the first 2 stitches on left needle **(Figure 1)**, wrap yarn around needle as if to knit, draw yarn through **(Figure 2)**, and place new loop on left needle **(Figure 3)** to form a new stitch. Repeat from * for the desired number of stitches, always working between the last 2 stitches made.

Figure 1

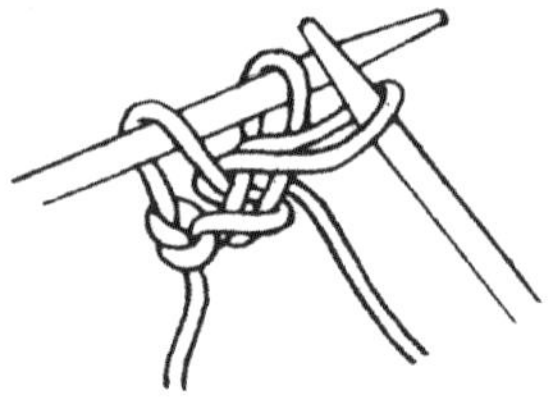

Figure 2

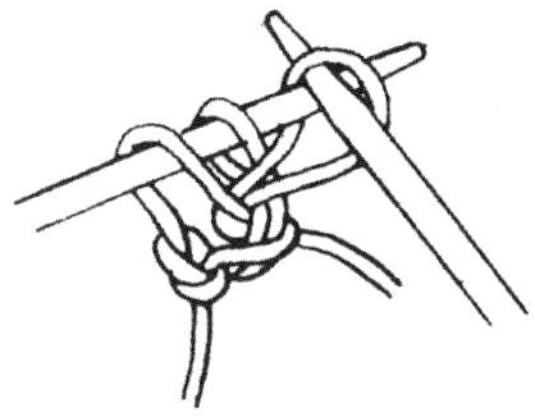

Figure 3

Knitted Cast-On

Make a slipknot and place it on the left needle if there are no stitches already there. *Use the right needle to knit the first stitch (or slipknot) on left needle **(Figure 1)** and place the new loop onto left needle to form a new stitch **(Figure 2)**. Repeat from * for the desired number of stitches, always working into the last stitch made.

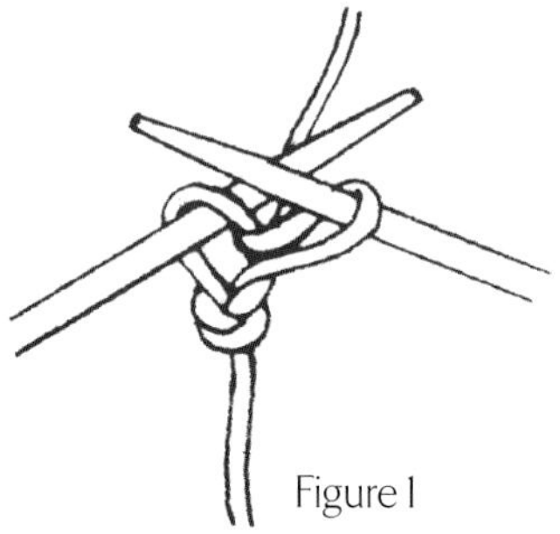

Figure 1

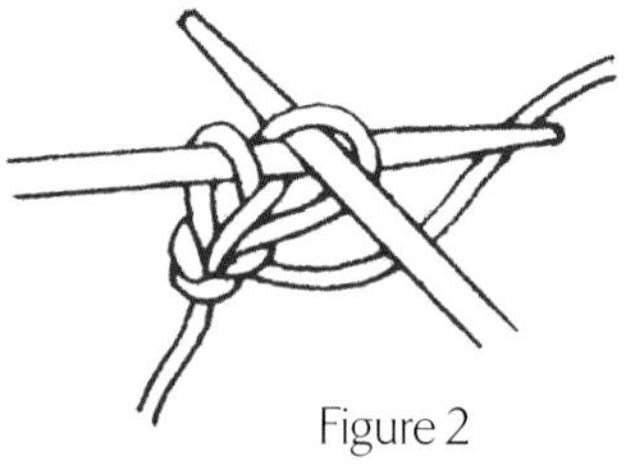

Figure 2

Tubular 1 × 1 Rib Cast-On

Leaving a long tail as for the long-tail method, make a slipknot and place on needle. Hold the tail end over your thumb and the ball end over your index finger **(Figure 1)**. The slipknot counts as the first stitch.

*Bring the needle around the strand on your index finger from back to front **(Figure 2)**, then bring the needle to the front and under the strand on your thumb **(Figure 3)**. Bring the needle back around the strand on your finger in the opposite direction so that the strand is below the needle and to the back **(Figure 4)**. Bring the needle under the thumb strand from front to back **(Figure 5)**. Bring the needle around the finger strand from back to front **(Figure 6)**. Bring the needle down under the thumb strand to the front **(Figure 7)**—2 stitches formed.

Repeat from *, adding 2 stitches every repeat, until there is 1 less stitch than desired. Bring the needle under the finger strand from front to back to create another loop on the needle, then tie the two strands of yarn together to secure **(Figure 8)**—there is an even number of stitches on the needle.

Begin working k1, p1 rib as follows:
Row 1: K1, *sl 1 pwise with yarn in front, k1 tbl; rep from *.
Row 2: K1, sl 1 pwise with yarn in front; rep from *.
Row 3 and subsequent rows: Work in k1, p1 rib as usual.

Figure 1

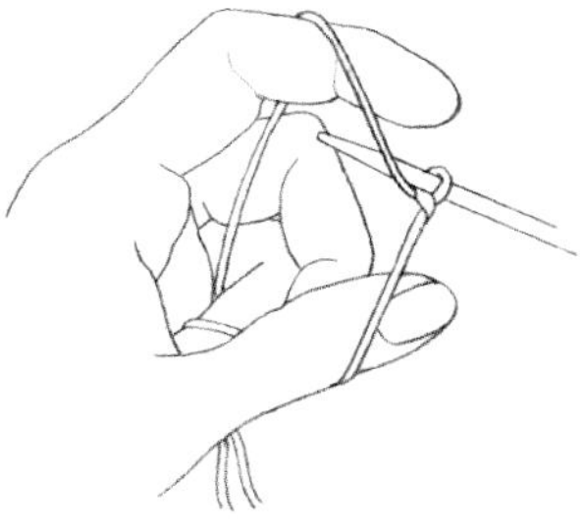
Figure 2

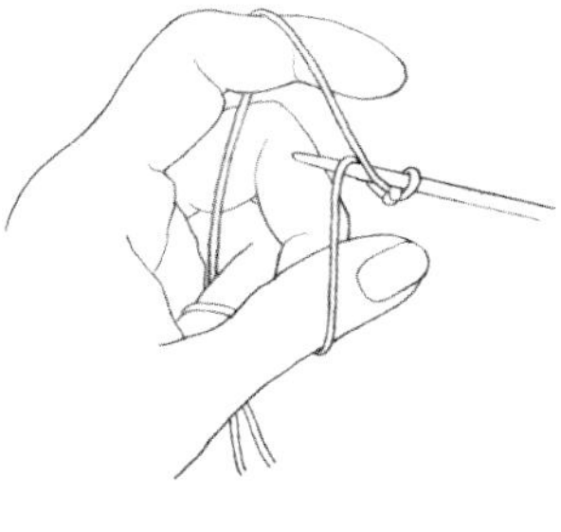
Figure 3

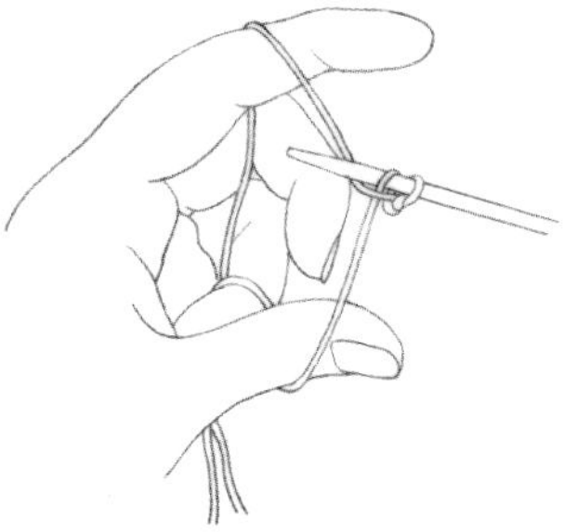
Figure 4

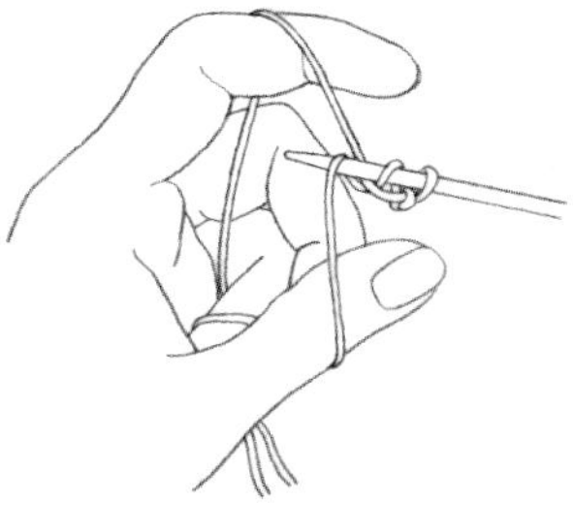
Figure 5

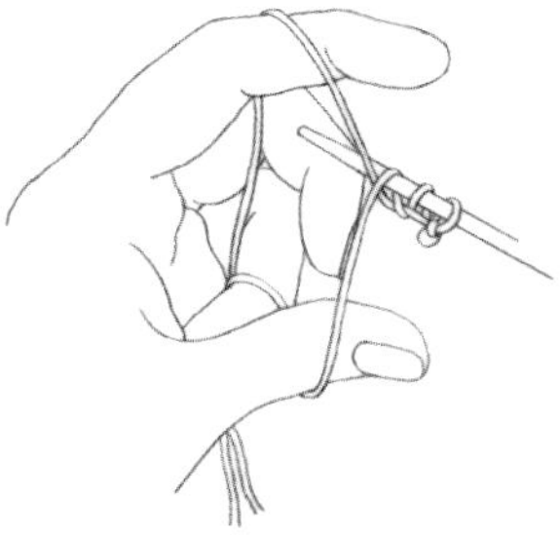
Figure 6

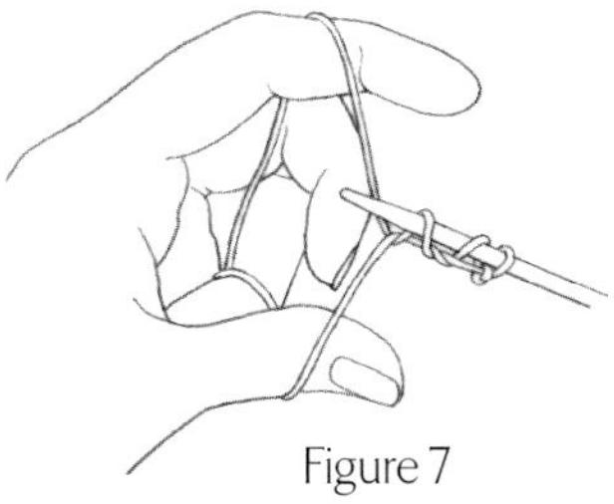
Figure 7

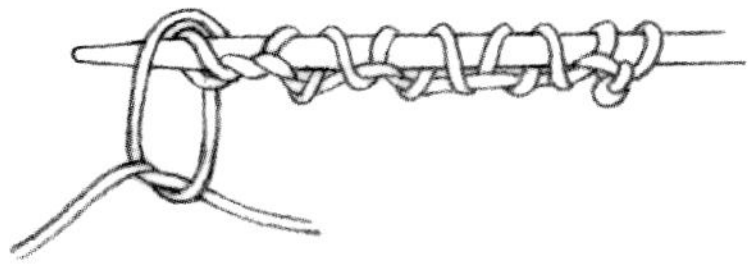
Figure 8

Long-Tail (Continental) Cast-On

Leaving a long tail (about ½" [1.3 cm] for each stitch to be cast on), make a slipknot and place on right needle. Place thumb and index finger of your left hand between the yarn ends so that working yarn is around your index finger and tail end is around your thumb and secure the yarn ends with your other fingers. Hold your palm upward, making a V of yarn **(Figure 1)**. *Bring needle up through loop on thumb **(Figure 2)**, catch first strand around index finger, and go back down through loop on thumb **(Figure 3)**. Drop loop off thumb and, placing thumb back in V configuration, tighten resulting stitch on needle **(Figure 4)**. Repeat from * for the desired number of stitches.

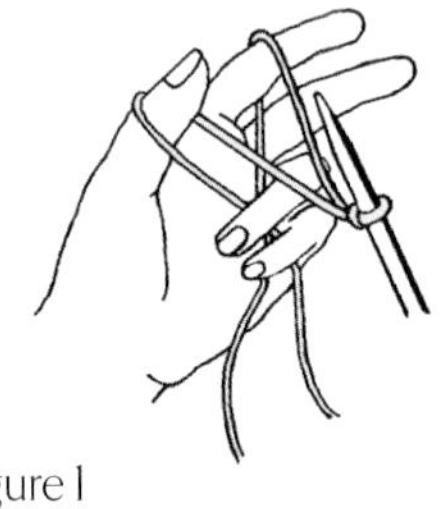

Figure 1

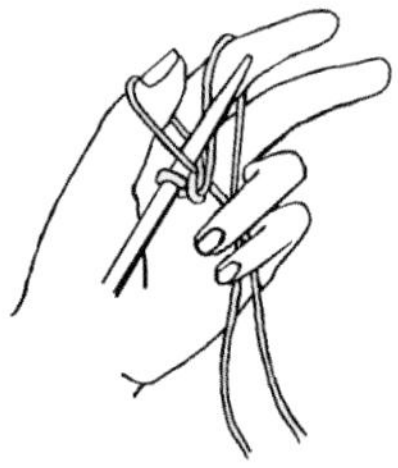

Figure 2

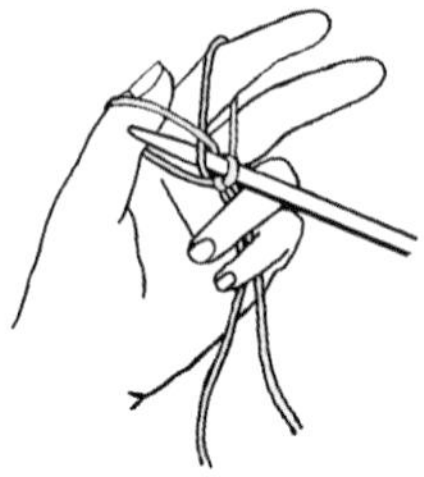

Figure 3

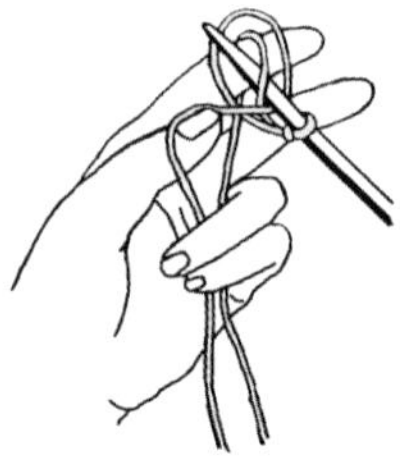

Figure 4

DECREASES

Knit 2 Together (k2tog)

Knit 2 stitches together as if they were a single stitch.

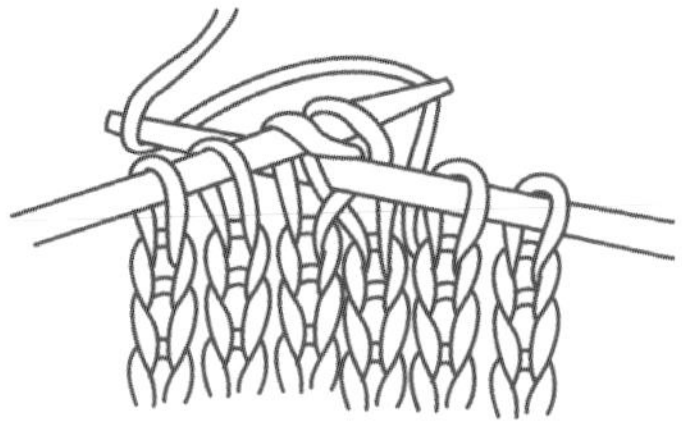

Slip, Slip, Knit (ssk)

Slip 2 stitches individually knitwise **(Figure 1)**, insert left needle tip into the front of these 2 slipped stitches, and use the right needle to knit them together through their back loops **(Figure 2)**.

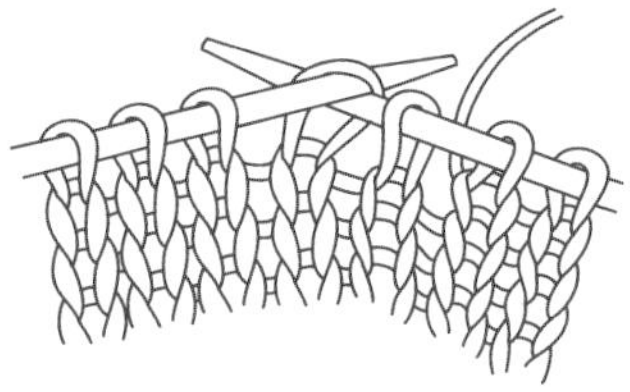

Figure 1

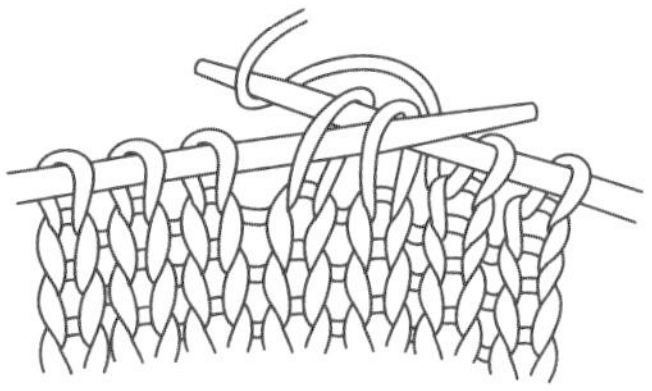

Figure 2

EMBROIDERY

Buttonhole Stitch

Working around the loop of yarn, *bring tip of threaded needle through the loop from front to back, place working yarn under needle tip, and tighten. Repeat from *, always bringing threaded needle on top of working yarn.

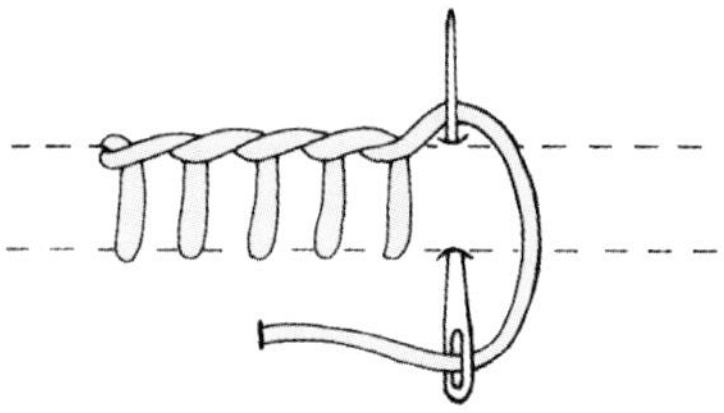

Duplicate Stitch

Bring threaded needle out from back to front at the base of the V of the knitted stitch you want to cover. *Working right to left, pass needle in and out under the stitch in the row above it and back into the base of the same stitch. Bring needle back out at the base of the V of the next stitch to the left. Repeat from * for the desired number of stitches.

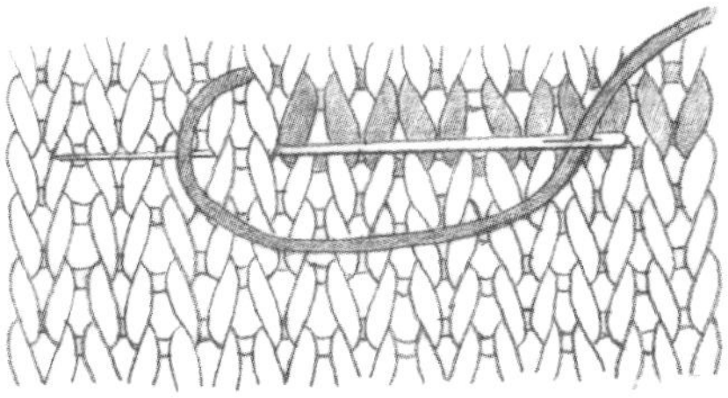

French Knot

Bring threaded needle out of knitted background from back to front, wrap yarn around needle one to three times, and use your thumb to hold the wraps in place while you insert needle into background a short distance from where it came out. Pull the needle through the wraps into the background.

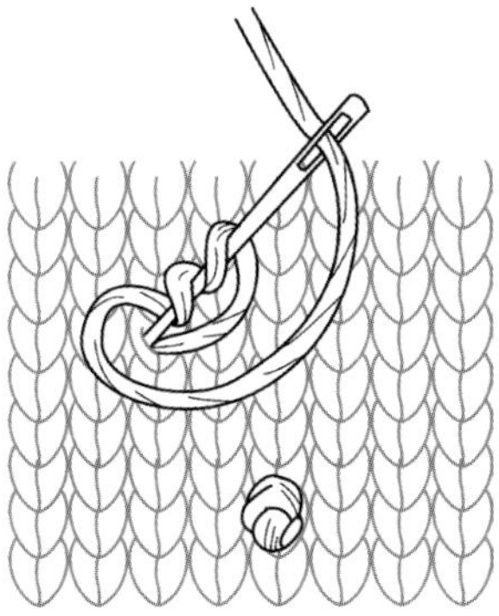

I-CORD (ALSO CALLED KNIT-CORD)

Use two double-pointed needles. Cast on the desired number of stitches (usually 3 to 5). Knit these stitches, then *without turning the work, slide stitches to other end of needle, pull the yarn around the back, and knit the stitches as usual. Repeat from * for the desired length.

INCREASES

Bar Increase (k1f&b)

Knit into a stitch but leave it on the left needle **(Figure 1)**, then knit through the back loop of the same stitch **(Figure 2)** and slip the original stitch off the needle **(Figure 3)**.

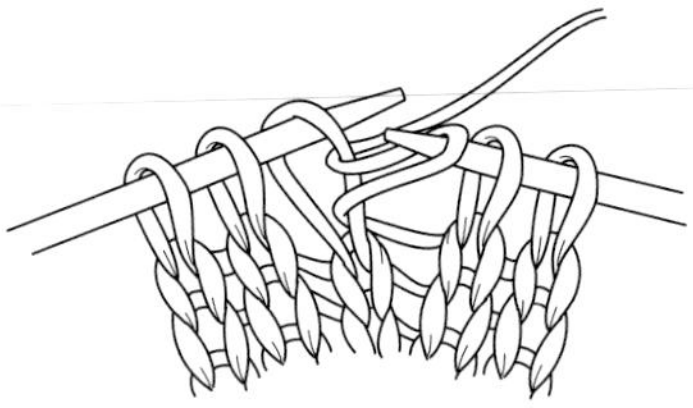

Figure 1

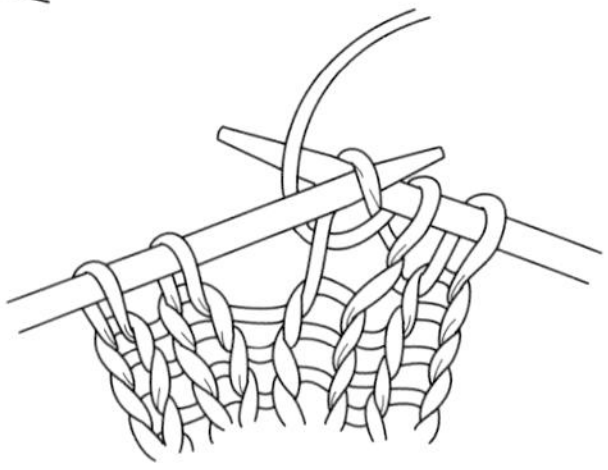

Figure 2

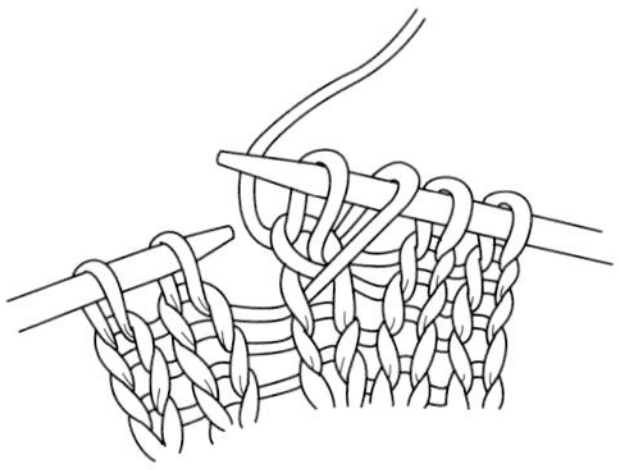

Figure 3

Raised Make One—Left Slant (M1L or M1)

Note: Use the left slant if no direction of slant is specified. With left needle tip, lift the strand between the last knitted stitch and the first stitch on the left needle from front to back **(Figure 1)**, then knit the lifted loop through the back **(Figure 2)**.

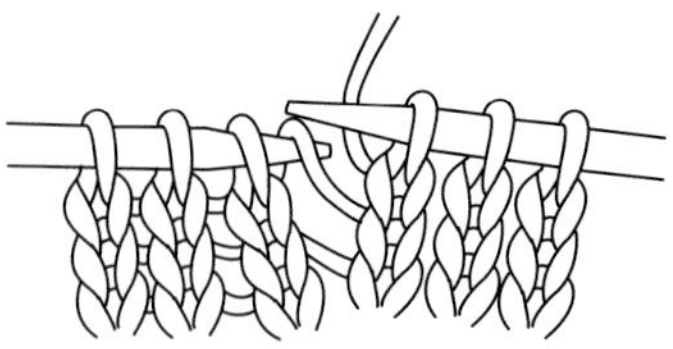

Figure 1

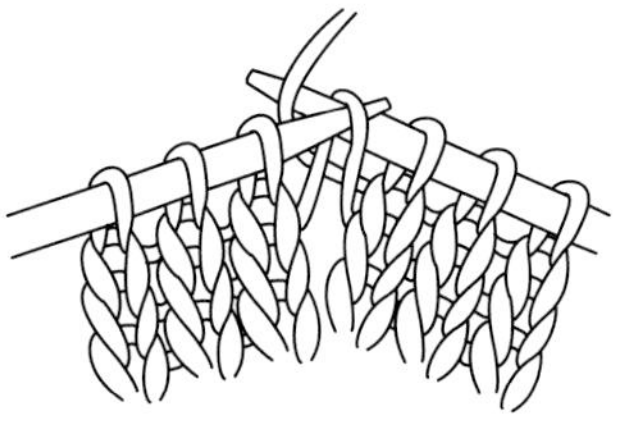

Figure 2

Raised Make One—Right Slant (M1R)

With left needle tip, lift the strand between the needles from back to front **(Figure 1)**. Knit the lifted loop through the front **(Figure 2)**.

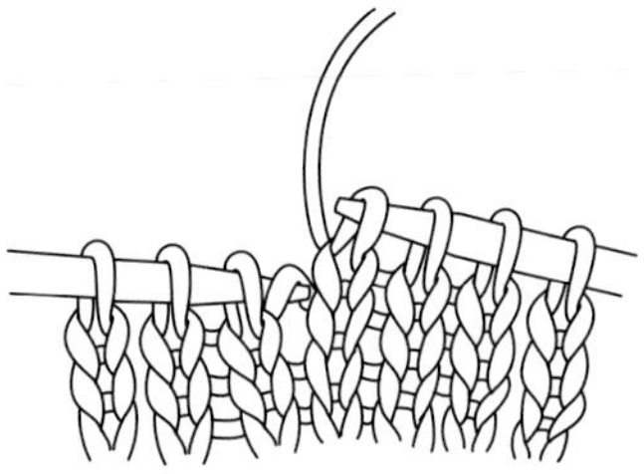

Figure 1

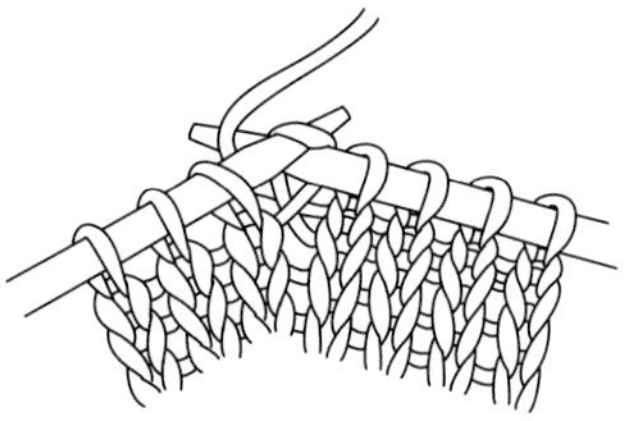

Figure 2

TWISTED CORD

Cut yarn about five times the desired finished cord length. Fold the strands in half. Anchor the strands at the fold by looping them over a doorknob. Twist the strands tightly in a clockwise direction until they begin to kink. Remove strands from doorknob, keeping tension on the strands. Bring the two ends together, allowing them to twist around each other counterclockwise. Smooth out the twists so that they are uniform along the length of the cord. Knot the ends.

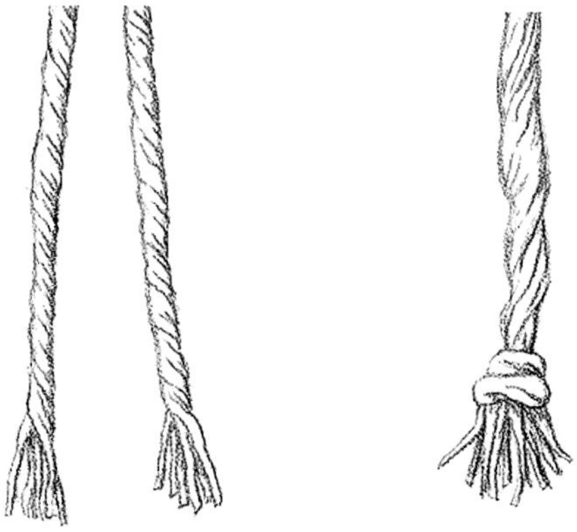

ZIPPER

With right side facing and zipper closed, pin zipper to the knitted pieces so edges cover the zipper teeth. With contrasting thread and right side facing, baste zipper in place close to teeth **(Figure 1)**. Turn work over and with matching sewing thread and needle, stitch outer edges of zipper to wrong side of knitting **(Figure 2)**, being careful to follow a single column of stitches in the knitting to keep zipper straight. Turn work back to right side facing, and with matching sewing thread, sew knitted fabric close to teeth **(Figure 3)**. Remove basting.

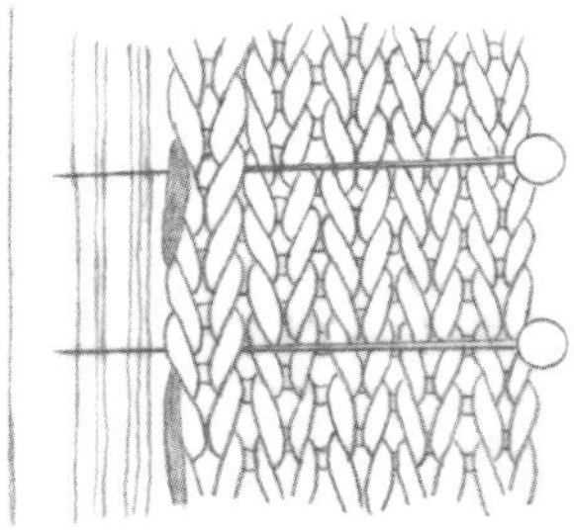

Figure 1

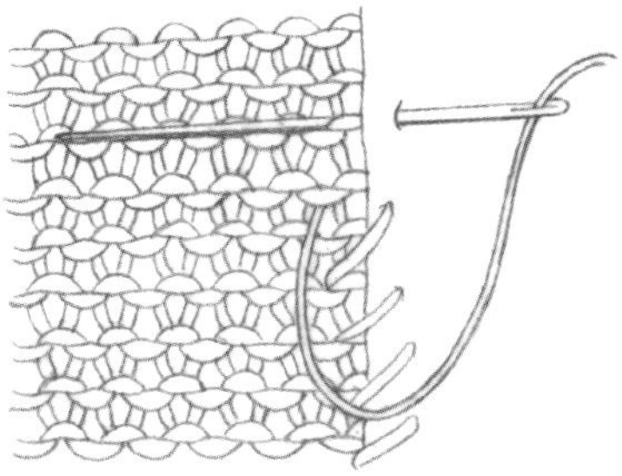

Figure 2

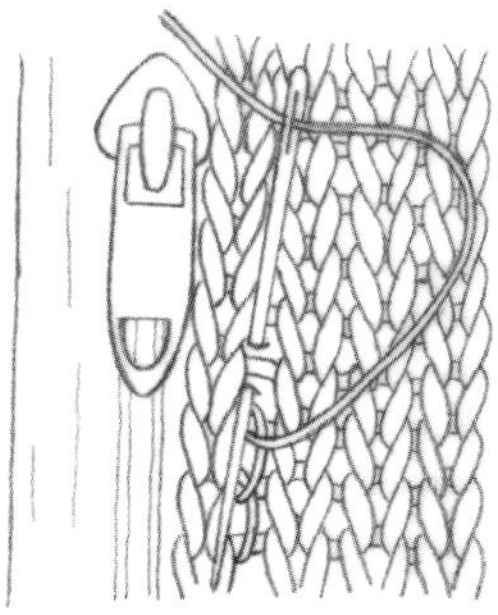

Figure 3

acknowledgments

To the all the creative minds at Interweave, I wish to extend my sincere appreciation. Particular thanks to Ann Budd, whose guidance has taught me so much, and Karen Frisa, for somehow translating what I wrote into what I really meant.

Linda Rhogaar; thank you for your expert advice and unwavering enthusiasm, despite the fact that my horse is often miles behind my cart.

My knitting friends and teachers are the geniuses upon whose shoulders I stand. Thank you for doing it first and showing me how. My heartfelt gratitude also belongs to the non-knitting Friends of Fitzgerald, at whose meetings I knitted all last summer. Your tolerance and frosty beverages helped more than you know.

Many thanks also to Katie Scott and Jane Wolff Scott for the loan of your skilled fingers; many hands make light the work. To Phillip, Lindsay, and Campbell, who never flinched when I gave up laundry in favor of art, I love you even more than yarn.

And to God, with whom all things are possible; thanks especially for making sheep.

resources

Arnhild's Knitting Studio/ Rauma
2315 Buchanan Dr.
Ames, IA 50010
arnhild.com

Blumenthal Lansing Co.
blumenthallansing.com

Brown Sheep
100662 County Rd. 16
Mitchell, NE 69357
brownsheep.com

Button Emporium & Ribbonry
1016 SW Taylor St.
Portland, OR 97205
buttonemporium.com

Classic Elite
122 Western Ave.
Lowell, MA 01851
classiceliteyarns.com

Creativity Inc./Blue Moon Beads
creativityinc.com

Dale of Norway
4750 Shelburne Rd., Ste. 20
Shelburne, VT 05482
dale.no

Diamond Yarn
9697 St. Laurent, Ste. 101
Montréal, QC
Canada H3L 2N1
and
155 Martin Ross, Unit 3
Toronto, ON
Canada M3J 2L9
diamondyarn.com

Dill Buttons
dillbuttons.com

Harrisville Designs
Center Village
PO Box 806
Harrisville, NH 03450
harrisville.com

Homestead Heirlooms
Pewaukee, WI
(262) 352-8738
homesteadheirlooms.com

JCA Inc./Reynolds
35 Scales Ln.
Townsend, MA 01469
jcacrafts.com

JHB International
1955 S. Quince St.
Denver, CO 80231
buttons.com

The Knitting Mills
PO Box 2125
Lynnwood, WA 98036
theknittingmills.com

Lion Brand Yarns
135 Kero Rd.
Carlstadt, NJ 07072
lionbrand.com

Louet North America/ Gems
808 Commerce Park Dr.
Ogdensburg, NY 13669
louet.com
in Canada:
3425 Hands Rd.
Prescott, ON K0E 1T0

Paradise Fibers
N. Thor St.
Spokane, WA 99202
paradisefibers.net

Scottish Country Shop
1450 SE Powell Blvd.
Portland, OR 97202
scottishcountryshop.com

Simply Shetland/Jamieson's
18375 Olympic Ave. S.
Seattle, WA 98188
simplyshetland.net

Tahki/Stacy Charles Inc./ Filatura di Crosa
70–30 80th St., Bldg. 36
Ridgewood, NY 11385
tahkistacycharles.com
in Canada: Diamond Yarn

index